Weddings *in* Color

Weddings *in* Color

500 Creative Ideas for Designing a Modern Wedding

Vané Broussard *and* Minhee Cho

Photographs by Jainé M. Kershner

Styling by Michelle Edgemont

CHRONICLE BOOKS

SAN FRANCISCO

For Chad and Tru x 2

Library of Congress Cataloging-in-Publication Data available.

ISBN 978-1-4521-3462-8

Manufactured in China

Designed by Allison Weiner and Amanda Sim

Styling by Michelle Edgemont

Alizé Bleu is a registered trademark of Kobrand Corporation. Bonne Maman is a registered trademark of
Andros Société en Nom Collectif. Domino is a registered trademark of Domino Sugar Corporation. Essie
is a registered trademark of L'Oreal USA Creative, Inc. Fresh is a registered trademark of LVMH. Grey
Goose is a registered trademark of Bacardi Global Brands Limited. HPNOTIQ is a registered trademark
of Heaven Hills Distilleries, Inc. Laduree is a registered trademark of Laduree International. Liquitex is
a registered trademark of ColArt Americas, Inc. Premo! Sculpey is a registered trademark of Polyform
Products Company, Inc.

10 9 8 7 6 5 4 3 2 1

Chronicle Books LLC
680 Second Street
San Francisco, California 94107
www.chroniclebooks.com

30540 Sycamore Street
San Diego, California
92104

Dearest,

Please mark your calendars and save the date
for the fifth of May, year 2016. We will
be exchanging vows on the sandy beach of
Ibiza, Spain. So pack your bags and get
ready to celebrate!

xoxo,

Marla and Kasey

p.s. more details to follow...

Contents

Foreword

I love how weddings have changed over the years. Of course, they're still about two people committing to one another, but what's different—and so exciting!—now is that when it comes to the look, feeling, and details, anything is possible. Minhee and Vané have been right in the thick of this style evolution, and in this book, they encourage engaged couples to get creative by illustrating the countless ways to personalize a celebration. And they make the process easy and fun! For example, they've organized the chapters by color, which is infinitely helpful as your palette is often the first thing you consider before diving into the details. After seeing many classic and vintage-inspired weddings, Minhee and Vané have developed their own style, knowing that weddings can be playful or sophisticated, eclectic or sexy. From a confetti bar to laser-cut invitations to a ring bearer walking a dog balloon down the aisle, their whimsical ideas inspire couples to add spirit and personality to their own weddings—or to any party, really, be it a shower, rehearsal dinner, or next-day brunch. This book shows just how modern and fun a very traditional day can be, and it's packed with so many ideas to help you get started and make your celebration a truly personal affair.

Congratulations to Minhee and Vané, who have been inspiring couples for years with their stationery and blog, and now, with this must-have resource for planning an unforgettable wedding.

Darcy Miller

DARCY MILLER
editorial director of *Martha Stewart Weddings*

Introduction

Resources for today's brides are out there, and they are plentiful, but they also tend to be one-note. And by one-note, we mean "vintage."

But what about brides who want a more modern look? A quick stroll around the wedding section of your local bookstore reveals key words like *rustic*, *romantic*, and *traditional* with images of princess ball gowns, pastel colors, and, of course, the ever-present mason jar! It seems most of today's wedding products are tailored to this particular aesthetic, leaving very little for the bride looking for something sleek and architectural.

Vané started her blog *Brooklyn Bride* to fill this hole in the wedding inspiration market. After getting engaged to her now-husband, Chad, and spending a few months researching weddings online, she realized that there was nothing out there for her modern tastes. It was all too pink and girly! So she started *Brooklyn Bride* as a way to collect her ideas. As people outside her immediate family started reading, she sensed she might be onto something. Soon, brides and grooms who were as devoted to the "modern wedding" cause as she was were following her. These days the blog is known for featuring real weddings from all over the world, showcasing vendors that subscribe to modern design ideals, and sharing a plethora of creative wedding ideas.

While planning *her* wedding in 2006, Minhee realized that timeless ideas can easily take a modern twist. For example, she had her bridesmaids wear wrist corsages and carry vintage-style clutches instead of traditional bouquets. The theme of her wedding was "old school," featuring blackboards and school furniture from the 1980s, but it was executed in a clean and modern style. Her wedding invitations were printed on old office paper with modern design touches mixed in. Given her creative work with Paper+Cup Design (the design studio she founded with her now-husband, Truman Cho, in 2003), she relished creating the overall design of the wedding, from paper to décor. It was through this initial

experience that Minhee recognized the importance of having a central theme for a wedding or event and building out from there. In 2006, her wedding was featured in *Martha Stewart Weddings*, launching many of the modern wedding trends we still see today.

So what *is* a modern wedding? This can be difficult to answer, because *modern* means different things to different people. To us, a modern wedding is an event that is crisp and clean with architectural details and minimal silhouettes. It is simple yet chic and doesn't take itself too seriously. Modern weddings go for bold, bright, and monochromatic color, and incorporate sleeker materials such as Lucite, lacquer, metals, and woods (but not the rough-hewn type).

The most defining aspect of a wedding (especially a modern wedding) is color. Color sets the mood for the entire affair. When choosing colors, think about what you want to convey to your guests. Do you want to go bright and cheerful for summer? Consider yellows, greens, or pinks in bold pops. Cozy and moody for autumn? Rich oranges and reds will work well and play off the seasonal hues. Look all around you for color inspiration. Brides these days have it a *lot* easier than brides of even just five years ago with the development of Pinterest and the growth of wedding blogs. Create boards of images in color palettes you like. Don't feel as if you have to look only at wedding-related sites. Some of the best color inspiration can come from fashion magazines, interior design books, graphic design publications, and even cookbooks. Create a mood board of colors, combinations, patterns, and textures that you want to see translated into your wedding. This will be the snapshot of your wedding style that you'll refer back to throughout the planning process, and it will help your vendors understand your vision.

Your own personal style will play a big role in color selection as well. Modern typically means a few bold, bright colors, and that's what you'll see in this book. Classic and traditional styles generally use a more muted palette, while vintage favors pastels. That's not to say that pastels can't work in modern color stories, though. Pairing pastels with their brighter counterparts or working them into geometric patterns will give them a modern spin!

To help with your color selection, we've arranged the book into eight color chapters. Each chapter presents a palette and a mood board to spark ideas. You'll notice that each color is paired minimally with white, and we do that for a reason: it's a universal color for weddings and also a great starting point for any palette. A clean, bright white is also incredibly modern, especially when paired with bold color. Within each chapter, you will find dozens of ideas for all the elements of a wedding: flowers, fashion, paper, food, and styling, along with an easy DIY project and a Q&A with a star wedding expert. While this book is divided by color, we hope you'll be inspired to translate an idea from the Blue/Purple chapter and make it green, or red, or whatever color palette works for you! Mix and match, layer, and expand on the ideas to make them your own. Our goal is to provide inspiration for an unforgettably modern wedding.

The rest is up to you!

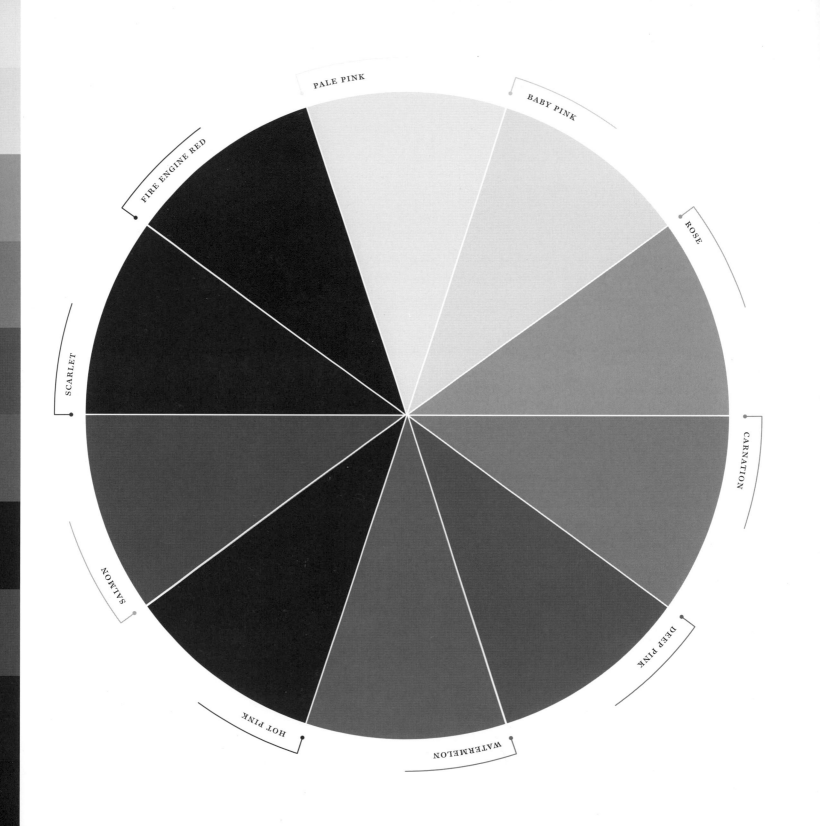

PALE PINK

BABY PINK

ROSE

FIRE ENGINE RED

CARNATION

SCARLET

DEEP PINK

SALMON

WATERMELON

HOT PINK

Palette

No color combination symbolizes love and affection more than red and pink.

It's no surprise, then, that this pair is one of the most popular for weddings. Red is the color of passion and excitement. It's also a real attention grabber. Remember Oprah's birthday celebration where she made everyone wear white and then came out in a red gown? All eyes were on her! It's an especially popular color in the winter months around the holidays, but it also works in autumn to coordinate with the changing leaves. We've seen it used during the warmer months in a bright hue like poppy or fire engine red. It is vibrant and fresh and brings life to a wedding. And it doesn't hurt that true red in particular is a universally flattering color, which means it photographs beautifully.

Pink, the softer sister of red, lends itself to a more romantic look. It comes in many shades from light to dark, pastel to electric, and each shade gives off a different vibe. Lighter pinks are decidedly more girly, perfect for all seasons and venues but especially prominent in the spring months. Hot pink has more energy and is great for brides who want a little more excitement while still staying feminine. Pink can work for styles from old world glamour to preppy to rock and roll with just the slightest change in hue, so its potential for variation is endless.

The Bouquet

It's not often that you get to carry a bouquet. So when you do, make sure it's a good one! Bouquets come in dozens of different styles, from nosegays to cascading to hand tied, not to mention all the different shapes and sizes. When meeting with your florist for the first time, bring pictures of your dress and inspirational images of bouquets you love. Having an image of your dress is important because your florist will be able to suggest the perfect size and shape for your bouquet, so that it complements the dress rather than competes with it. Discuss the colors you envision and make sure you're aware of which flowers will be available at the time of your wedding. Ideally, you want to select flowers that are in season when you're getting married so that you don't get your heart set on the impossible. And get

ABOVE: When it comes to bouquets, having a tonal variety of the same color makes for a more visually appealing bouquet, while bringing in a color or pattern to the ribbon also adds some excitement.

The best flowers are selected for the bride's bouquet in particular because she'll be carrying and looking at them all day! This asymmetrical hand-tied bouquet is a common style for weddings.

ready to be shocked by the price of the good stuff! Some blooms can be $10 or more for a single flower, and typically, a bridal bouquet will cost $275 to $300 alone.

The bride's bouquet tends to be larger than those for the bridesmaids, and it uses the highest quality blooms. Bridesmaids generally have the same flowers, just in differing quantities, unless the bride really wants to stand out and go with a completely different color or shape. If you want to get deep into the symbolism of certain blooms or you have your heart set on one in particular, let your florist know so he or she can work it into the design. For example, roses are symbolic for love, and stephanotis typically mean marital happiness, so these flowers are very popular for weddings.

Some flowers, as beautiful as they are, however, just aren't the best for wedding bouquets. Lily of the valley is incredibly beautiful and fragrant, but it doesn't last very long before starting to droop. That doesn't stop some brides from using it, but you should be aware of this ahead of time. Similarly, hydrangeas need a lot of water to stay fresh looking, so they're not ideal for bouquets (but they work well for centerpieces). Be sure to understand the care your bouquet flowers need before finalizing your choice.

Before the big day, you might want to do some bicep curls to prepare because a decent-sized bouquet can be heavy! When walking down the aisle, some brides tend to hold the bouquet up high, but the best place is actually just below your waist. Relax your hands, let your elbows pop out to the sides slightly, and tilt the bouquet forward a bit.

What to do with your bouquet after the wedding? At the end of the evening, some brides like to take part in the traditional bouquet toss. However, not everyone wants to toss her beautiful bouquet! You can instead save your main bouquet as a keepsake and ask your florist to make a small "toss bouquet" for the occasion also. But even a toss bouquet won't come free, so make sure to add this additional cost into your budget. If you plan on preserving bits of your bouquet for memory's sake, you can pull out a couple of flowers that you want to save and hang them upside down in a protected spot for a few weeks until they are perfectly dry. If you'd like to press them, place the blooms between two sheets of newspaper or tissue and then press them in a heavy book until they are dry.

OPPOSITE: You can see how many different flower varieties it can take to make up one bouquet. The bouquet on the preceding page uses more than eight, including two types of tulips and peonies, to make it visually interesting within a single color palette.

Parrot tulip

Garden roses

Tulip

Coral charm peony

Ixia

Cirsium

Peony

Veronica

Lisianthus

Ranunculus

Bouvardia

Wedding day makeup

FASHION

Your wedding day makeup is important because you want to look your very best but also have your natural beauty shine through. Wedding day beauty is all about balance, but there's absolutely no reason you can't experiment with some pops of color since all eyes will be on you for the day! For example, if you're going for a bold lip, then you want to tone down your eyes and cheeks. That doesn't mean you can't use any eye makeup; instead, just make sure to keep your eye makeup more subtle and pair it with some waterproof mascara and dark eyeliner. If you'd rather play up your cheekbones, then go for some rosy blush and tone down everything else.

When it comes to picking the actual colors, test out a few ahead of time. Your makeup artist will be able to recommend good colors for your skin tone at your trial makeup session, but here are some quick tips: if you're fair skinned, stay away from lip or eye makeup that has a brown undertone. Orangey red shades will look great with your skin, and blue-based red lipsticks will make your teeth look whiter! Medium-skinned ladies can also do pinks and corals but use them in deeper shades. Darker skin tones handle pigmented bright colors well, especially raspberry pinks, oranges, and translucent reds. Bright colors will make you look youthful and confident, and most important, happy.

OPPOSITE: Bold cheeks give off a youthful vibe, perfect for a daytime wedding.

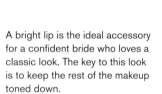

A bright lip is the ideal accessory for a confident bride who loves a classic look. The key to this look is to keep the rest of the makeup toned down.

Lipsticks and blushes in a variety of pinks and reds for every skin tone. The bolder the better! Depending on what kind of look you're going for, your nails can enjoy some color too, whether a deep cabernet or the palest of pinks.

Unique invitations

In the Black chapter (pages 150 to 175), we cover the traditional methods of printing for invitations. Here, we're focusing on unique invitations. If you love paper as much as we do, you know how much fun it is to get a nontraditional invitation in the mail. It generates buzz and excitement about the event and becomes an instant keepsake. Thinking of new and different ways to use paper (or not using paper at all!) leads to a lot of fun opportunities with invitation design.

If you want to stick with the tried-and-true paper invitation, consider the shape as a way to be unique. A lot of companies will die-cut shapes for you—everything from hearts to triangles to faceted polygons. You'll still be able to use traditional printing techniques on a die-cut invitation, but the die-cutting process itself will be an additional cost, especially if a custom die needs to be made. To offset that cost, stick with less expensive printing techniques such as offset or digital. Your invitations can also take an interactive turn with simple crafting techniques such as adding grommets or brads to make fortune-teller-inspired invites or providing paper dolls that your guests can dress up for fun.

For non-paper invitations, your options are limitless. Dollar-store toys with a little note attached are a sweet token of celebration and easy enough to mail in a bubble pouch envelope. Laser cutting is becoming increasingly popular and can be done in color with acrylic or on wood for a more natural look. Printing your invitation onto fabric makes a lasting impression and can do double duty as men's hankies or for the ladies to use to wipe away tears of joy at the wedding. Just remember that the more bulk in the envelope, the higher the postage cost, so you'll need to take this into account in your overall invitation budget.

OPPOSITE: Forget the paper and have the words become the actual invitation with these laser-cut acrylic typographic invitations.

RSVP
BY THE TENTH OF JUNE

TOGETHER WITH THEIR PARENTS

JOANNA & OLIVER

INVITE YOU TO JOIN THEM IN A

Celebration

OF MARRIAGE
SATURDAY, THE TENTH OF OCTOBER
TWO THOUSAND FOURTEEN
HALF PAST FOUR IN THE AFTERNOON

BEAULIEU GARDENS
NAPA, CALIFORNIA
BLACK TIE ATTIRE

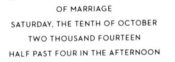

There's nothing cuter than an interactive invitation featuring paper dolls of the couple! Normally, whimsy like this is reserved for the save-the-date notice, but why not bring a little fun to the invitation itself?

Have guests take your invitation for a spin to find out all the details in this fun take on a fortune-teller.

A little plastic horn turns a regular invitation into something to celebrate. Encourage your guests to bring the horns to the ceremony to toot as you head back down the aisle!

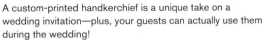

A custom-printed handkerchief is a unique take on a wedding invitation—plus, your guests can actually use them during the wedding!

Die-cut invitation suites may be a little on the pricey side, but they definitely make up for it with originality.

Beyond the cake

Even though cakes are the traditional dessert for the couple to share during their reception, lots of couples don't want that for their wedding. Thankfully, you have so many other delicious options these days that guests barely even notice if the cake is missing. One popular alternative is pies. Who doesn't love a variety of yummy pies with a scoop of vanilla ice cream or a dollop of fresh whipped cream? Pie is comfort food—and it's especially perfect for outdoor weddings.

Other options are cake pops or individual cake cups. Just don't confuse cake cups with cupcakes! These darling mini cakes are assembled into glass cups that can then double as favors for your guests. You can display either to look like a wedding cake, and another nice thing is that you can offer far more flavors than you can with just one cake. Cream puffs and macarons can be displayed similarly, and they make a stunning centerpiece for a dessert table. And don't forget the humble donut! Always delicious, donuts can be dressed up or down in any and every color and come in dozens of flavors, making them totally versatile. The nice thing about all of these options is that you can still work a cake topper into the design, and your actual dessert can double as an edible takeaway favor at the end of the reception if packaged appropriately.

OPPOSITE: Mini cheesecakes with fresh red berries are a delicious alternative to the wedding cake. Strawberries make great toppers because they're naturally shaped like hearts!

Cake pops! They're bite-sized, make no mess, and are great for kids and adults alike.

Homemade cupcakes can look extra professional with the addition of ready-made fondant toppers.

Stack those mini-donuts high for an impressive display of sugary sweetness. Choose different colors, flavors, and toppings for fun variation.

Cake cups take the best part of a wedding cake and make it infinitely easier to transport (and eat!). If you customize the glass, it can double as a distinctive wedding favor.

Pink petit fours are a sweet little treat at the end of night and look adorable, too.

For all the pie lovers out there, display a bunch of your favorite flavors on cake stands in varying heights for an interesting display. And feel free to add cake toppers or flags for a festive feel.

STYLING
Aisle runners

It's still rare to see a wedding that doesn't make use of an aisle runner, but in all actuality, they're hardly needed. This custom first began during a time when roads weren't paved and guests would trample dirt and mud into the church. The aisle runner was a way to protect the bride's dress as she walked down the aisle.

These days, an aisle runner is pretty much just a decorative element, but many weddings incorporate it in one of two common ways: as a single piece of material down the center of the aisle, or as loose elements (like flower petals) down the center or down the edges of the aisle. While not entirely necessary, a runner works well to define the aisle, especially if your ceremony is set up in a way that doesn't clearly define that space.

Aisle runners made of a single piece of material are generally rolled out just before the bride is about to make her walk down the aisle. This typically serves as a signal for the guests to rise and for the processional music to change. If you use an aisle runner, make sure that the material isn't super slick and is tacked down properly. You don't want to risk slipping or tripping when everyone has their eyes on you! If you choose to use loose elements, you will need to have those laid out as soon as all the other décor elements—and guests!—are in place. Make sure your venue is okay with the use of petals, sequins, or other small pieces before planning on those. Likewise, lit candles in tall hurricane candleholders can also be incredibly beautiful, especially for an evening wedding, but again, you will want to check with your venue about using them.

OPPOSITE: There's no reason your aisle runner has to be plain. A graphic pattern helps you make a big entrance.

M & A

These aisle runners are anything but the usual! Whether you use custom-printed or dip-dyed fabric or a piece of material with handmade tassels along the edge, you can have a runner that will definitely direct all eyes to you as you head down the aisle.

Smaller elements such as a sprinkling of sequins or flower petals are equally striking as nontraditional runners.

An aisle runner doesn't have to be a roll of fabric down the center of the aisle. Elements along the sides of the aisle can also delineate your path, such as these die-cut letters and inexpensive flagging tape in multiple patterns.

Painted birdcage veil

If a plain white veil just won't cut it for your stylish ways, a fun option to add some color is to use paint! This project takes an inexpensive ready-made veil and makes it totally unique.

WHAT YOU'LL NEED:

- One 12-by-24-in/30.5-by-61-cm sheet of wax paper (plus extra)
- 1 roll artist's or masking tape
- 1 tube acrylic paint in your chosen color
- Ready-made birdcage veil with a tight weave (any length will work)

- One ¾-in/2-cm diameter sponge dabber (We used one from a Martha Stewart multipack, but you can also use a variety of sizes.)
- Bottle or similar prop to lean your veil against to dry

1. Lay out the wax paper, taping down the edges with the artist's tape.
2. Squeeze a dab of paint onto one corner of the wax paper. Make sure that the paint is in an area of the wax paper that won't come in contact with the birdcage veil.
3. Fan out the birdcage veil on the wax paper so you have a flat section of it to work with and tape down the edges with the artist's tape to prevent it from shifting. Using the sponge dabber, pick up a little bit of paint and dab it onto the veil. Dab in the same spot a couple of times to make sure that the paint makes a perfect circle and that the veil material is saturated. Continue making dots in a small area of the veil but make sure not to shift the veil as you work or the paint from the wax paper underneath will smear and transfer to other areas of the veil.

4. Lift up the veil and make sure you've got perfect circles. If some circles need a little more attention, carefully lay the veil back down and do a couple more dabs of the paint.
5. Let the veil dry on a tall bottle and change out the wax paper before beginning a new section. The paint dries relatively quickly, but allow 15 minutes between painting sessions just in case.
6. Repeat steps 3 through 5 until you have the design you want. Try on the veil as you go to make sure you're getting the pattern you want.
7. Let the veil dry completely, and you've got a beautifully patterned birdcage veil!

Ask the expert

LINSEY WACHALTER OF FACE TIME BEAUTY

Linsey Snyder Wachalter worked with some of the biggest names in Hollywood during her three-season stint as a makeup artist with *Saturday Night Live*. Taking her passion to the next level, she started Face Time Beauty where she and her team focus on everything beauty related, from brides to Broadway. While continuing to grow her business, she frequently works on special projects and with celebrities.

Q: How far ahead should brides start prepping their skin before the big day?

A: Ideally, you want to start your skin regimen as soon as you get engaged, but starting at least one month before will give you time to get your skin into shape.

Q: What are some secret tips you can recommend?

A: Always drink lots of water to get rid of toxins. Exercise regularly—working out not only helps you feel fit but actually clears skin. Exfoliate three times a week and moisturize every night before bed. If you choose to get a facial, be sure to get this done at least three days before the big day so your skin has a chance to settle down.

Q: What are some timeless bridal makeup styles?

A: All makeup styles can be tweaked a bit to look modern. A soft smoky eye and soft pink lip is always classic and beautiful. A sun-kissed face with full lashes and a neutral lip color is great for an effortless vibe. A red lip can read very Audrey Hepburn, which of course is perfect for the classic bride. The best makeup look ultimately is the one that the bride is most comfortable and confident in.

Q: What trends should brides stay away from?

A: Anything eighties! No French twists! No bright purple shadow! Keep it modern with a soft and whimsical vibe.

Q: Do you really need a makeup or hair trial before?

A: It's best to meet with your hairstylist and makeup artist before the big day. This way you can assess whether they are a good fit personally and professionally. You want to be sure you vibe with your beauty team and that they produce a look that you feel good in.

Q: How far ahead should brides schedule the trial?

A: As far ahead as possible! You want to leave enough time to find someone else if you are not happy with your first encounter. Another plus to starting early with a beauty team is that it allows time for a second or even a third meeting. Our brides tend to have a few parties before the big day—such as the engagement party and shower—and they can hire their team for these events, too. The more you work with your team, the more comfortable everyone will be on the wedding day.

Q: How should you figure out the best hairstyle for your dress and/or veil?

A: You first should decide what you are most comfortable with, hair up or hair down. Then find a few pictures for inspiration. Look online and search your favorite celebrity to see how she wore her hair at different red-carpet events. Pinterest and wedding blogs are great for inspiration and ideas. Once you have some sort of an idea, reach out to a beauty company and set a trial. Try to set a trial on the same day you have a fitting. This way you can see both hair and makeup with the dress.

Q: What should brides keep with them the day of for touch-ups?

A: Our favorite touch-up tool is the angle sponge. Use this to wipe off any excess makeup that has fallen on the skin or smudged. Always keep lip gloss or lipstick with you and blotting papers if you tend to get oily. We never suggest using too much powder because by the end of the night it will look cakey. We always say the best touch-up is taking off makeup instead of putting on more.

Q: Quick fire: Neutral or pop of color?

A: Pop of color. I think a neutral palette with a bright color on lips or cheeks is youthful and vibrant. It shows your guests you are having fun.

Q: Quick fire: Updo or down?

A: Down. If you take good care of your hair, let it shine! We love extensions if you need to add length. Be sure to get real hair extensions and match the color perfectly.

Q: Quick fire: Fake tan, bronzer, or no tan?

A: Light fake tan. It's always better to glow a little, especially against a white dress. It makes you look and feel alive.

Q: If you were a color, what color would you be?

A: Fuchsia. It says fun, flirty, romantic, vibrant, and modern all at the same time!

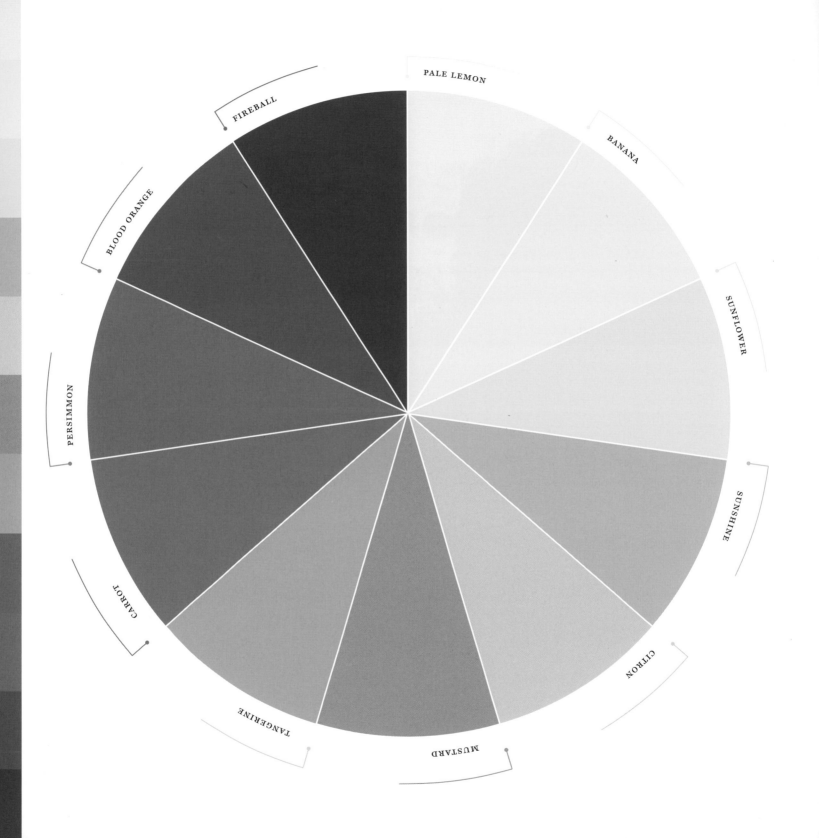

PALE LEMON

BANANA

SUNFLOWER

SUNSHINE

CITRON

MUSTARD

TANGERINE

CARROT

PERSIMMON

BLOOD ORANGE

FIREBALL

Palette

Yellow and orange are the happiest colors on the spectrum to choose for your wedding. Yellow in particular is a cheerful color, with shades ranging from pale butter to ultra-bright acid yellow to darker tones like mustard. Not surprising, it is a popular choice for weddings during the spring and summer months, but it also fits with autumn when the leaves are changing since it works so nicely with reds and oranges. Yellow makes flower selection easy because there are so many varietals out there in all different shades, such as daffodils and sunflowers. Pairing yellow with different colors can totally change its look . . . yellow and blue make a great nautical theme, while lemon and lime are a perfect summer punch. You will find some pitfalls with yellow, though. While it pairs well with neutrals like gray and white, team it up with black and you risk the bumblebee effect. Also, going overboard with yellow, especially in the wrong shade, can drape everyone in an unflattering light and make pictures look a bit sallow. Yellow works best as a bold accent.

Orange is another one of those "look at me" colors with an endless array of shades. Peach, coral, poppy, tangerine . . . even the names sound happy and summery! Orange goes well with many colors including hot pink, bright green, navy, and, of course, our favorite neutrals, gray and white. But as with yellow, keep it away from black. Orange is an ideal color for outdoor weddings, and it also can liven up indoor venues, especially in its brighter shades. It's commonly found in modern urban weddings as an accent color, which just proves how versatile and appealing it really is.

Ceremony flowers

Ceremony flowers are an important detail for your wedding because they dress up the space where you get married and so will end up being the backdrop of almost all your ceremony photos. It's also the first hint at what the reception will look like.

In general, you will need flowers in two main areas: the aisle and the altar. For church or synagogue weddings, it's easy to put freestanding floral arrangements at the altar. If you're getting married at a venue that doesn't have an altar, consider using florals to create the illusion of one. A chuppah or fabric backdrop flanked by arrangements can turn an otherwise unfinished space into a beautiful focal point for the ceremony. A creative take on the altar backdrop is to use oversized balloons and, instead of tying them to a simple string, attach them to a floral garland. Your florist will have to experiment with the weight of the flowers (they start adding up, no matter how small they are), but it's a unique look. Another creative idea is to place floral arrangements on stacked clear acrylic boxes. This will give the impression that the arrangements are floating and is a decidedly more modern way to frame an "altar" space.

You will want to dress up the aisle, too. Whether you sprinkle loose petals down the aisle or attach small arrangements to the chairs lining the way, it's important to make a lovely path to the altar. Instead of traditional arrangements, you can opt for potted plants or arrangements of branches (just make sure they are seasonally appropriate and don't block anyone's view of the ceremony). Arrangements can also be reused at the reception. For example, altar arrangements could find new homes at the escort card table or even next to the bar during cocktail hour.

You can find other opportunities to use flowers in your ceremony setting, such as a garland draping a welcome sign, a wreath hung on the door where guests enter, or simply blooms popped into the holes of a pegboard holding your wedding programs. Ultimately, it all comes down to your budget, what your venue allows, and how big of a statement you want to make.

Signs welcoming your guests can get the floral treatment, too. Try a ready-made garland with bright blooms tucked into it.

Hang floral garlands in a creative way by stringing them to a few oversized balloons for a festive ceremony backdrop.

Poppies make a festive addition to this pegboard.

Lining your aisle with larger floral arrangements makes for a grand entrance.

Himmeli ornaments in varying sizes and shapes are the perfect vessel for hanging airplants. Consider hanging a bunch above a ceremony altar or as a photo booth backdrop.

Veils & fascinators

FASHION

Veils are so steeped in tradition that sometimes it's hard to imagine a bride getting married without one. But it can be a little tricky finding the right one, especially given all the styles and ideas out there. Start your search by looking through magazines and websites to find styles of veils that you like. Pay close attention to face shapes that are similar to yours to get an idea of how a particular veil would look on you. Do you want a veil that's short and flirty like a birdcage or one that is cathedral length à la Princess Diana? Also take a look at the types of hairstyles worn with the particular veils you're looking at. Does your veil of choice look best with hair down or up?

When you start shopping for the veil, bring a snippet sample of your gown fabric if you can. Tulle, the most common material for veils, comes in a variety of colors, so you'll want to make sure it complements the dress. Don't feel as if you need to stick with whites or ivories, though. We've seen veils in pale pinks and blues that work perfectly, too! If your dress has a lot of beading or detailing, opt for a simple veil. If your dress is free of embellishment, then look into veils that have lace or ribbon edging, crystals, or beads as detailing. For drama, go with something oversized like a large pouf, or for a modern look, choose a blusher (otherwise known as a birdcage veil) in a bold color.

Fascinators are excellent alternatives to traditional veils. Less cumbersome, they can add great whimsy and color to your look. They're incredibly common at events in the United Kingdom, especially among wedding guests, but brides can rock these statement pieces, too. Just be sure to choose one in colors that complement your bouquet. If you think your fascinator is too bold for the ceremony and all of your pictures, you can always wear a simple veil for the ceremony and don the fascinator at the reception!

OPPOSITE: Fascinators are certainly not for the faint of heart, but they make quite the fashion statement as a veil alternative!

A standard veil gets a bit of a color pop thanks to some bright flowers tucked behind the ear.

A simple ring of fabric posies looks great on its own or when paired with a simple veil.

This feather headpiece paired with a vintage bit of yellow veiling makes a subtle statement while still adding a pop of color.

An oversized pouf of a veil is the ultimate accessory for an urban bride.

Go for bold with this neon orange blusher. It's the perfect addition to an architecturally detailed dress.

1

2

3

PAPER
Programs

Ceremonies can be full of rituals and customs that may leave some guests scrambling to keep up. When do we stand? What are the lyrics to this song? Who is that up there reading a passage? A program guides your guests through the ceremony and is a vital part of the affair.

Wedding programs come in many forms, but they generally include the same type of information: your names; wedding date, location, and order of the ceremony; names of the people in the bridal party and their relationship to you; names of readers; and the officiant's name. If musical selections are meaningful to you, consider including the lyrics of songs so that guests can follow along easily, as well as any explanations of traditions and customs that make an appearance. End the program with a note of thanks to both sets of parents and a remembrance of deceased loved ones if you wish.

When it comes to actually making and personalizing a program, the sky's the limit! Go with an elegant one- or two-sided program and bring meaningful details into the design. Or, for an outdoor wedding, you may consider making your program in the form of a fan to perform double duty. If your wedding is superformal, a scroll tied with beautiful ribbon may be more your style. Feel free to add photos, quotes, poems, or anything else that's personal to you. Either have an usher hand them out or set up baskets at the ends of the aisles for guests to take a program as they enter. You could also ask a couple of friends to place programs at each chair so that they are ready when guests take their seats.

4

1: Stylized doves keep this classic one-sided program chic and modern. **2:** Fan programs are perfect for outdoor weddings since they perform double duty by keeping your guests cool and informed! **3:** An accordion-folded program is an elegant alternative to the standard program, and it is still nice and compact. **4:** These composition book programs are a great example of working your theme (in this case, an "old school" theme) into various elements of your wedding.

WEDDING CEREMONY

PROCESSIONAL

CALL TO WORSHIP

STATEMENT OF INTENT

the wedding ceremony for

Vivian Hong & Edward Han
saturday, the seventh of november
two thousand fifteen

the wedding ceremony for

Vivian Hong & Edward Han
saturday, the seventh of november
two thousand fifteen

We absolutely love this confetti program idea!
One side of the aisle gets one color, and the other
side gets another color. When the ceremony is
finished, all of the guests toss confetti, and the
colors combine in the air!

please take a
CONFETTIGRAM

■ BRIDE

◆ GROOM

FOOD
Cold desserts

For summer weddings, especially those held outdoors, nothing is more refreshing for guests than a cold treat to keep the heat at bay. We've seen cold desserts served with wedding cakes, as alternatives to cakes, or just as an added bonus at the end of the night, so it's up to you how to work them in. A cold dessert bar is a unique alternative to the popular candy dessert table, and fun for guests of all ages. Because it can be a little difficult to keep items cold, you'll want to have someone manning the table and replenishing melting reserves often. For an ice cream bar, choose a couple of classic flavors along with all the best toppings from sprinkles to hot fudge to the requisite cherry on top. Cones in customized wrappers or cups in colors coordinated to your wedding theme will tie it all together, no matter the flavor.

Alternatives to traditional scoops of ice cream are plentiful and just as tasty. Gourmet popsicles artfully dipped in toppings, snow cones or shaved ice with an assortment of syrups, ice cream sandwiches with customized wrappers, even frozen fruit dipped in chocolate are all fun options as dessert offerings to your guests. If it all seems a little daunting to coordinate and you'd rather leave it to the professionals, hire an ice cream truck or popsicle cart to come and set up shop at your venue. It's guaranteed to bring a sweet bit of nostalgia to the night.

OPPOSITE: Attach some clip art tags to your popsicle sticks for an added graphic element.

CLAIRE and ETHAN

MR.

C • E

CHEERS TO THE HAPPY COUPLE • K

CLAIRE and ETHAN

MRS.

Dress up ice cream cones with customizable wraps to help with mess and keep everything colorful.

For an outdoor wedding, these paper plates, napkins, and ice cream bowls are the perfect pop of color for any cold dessert.

A Champagne float is an easy yet sophisticated update on the ice cream float, and it is perfect for a wedding on a warm summer night. You can also offer a nonalcoholic version using ginger ale.

Sprinkles in colors corresponding to your theme are the perfect way to dress up ice cream or cold desserts. And don't forget: the cherry on top can come in colors other than red, too!

Sorbets served in fruit "bowls" made from the actual fruits offer a perfect presentation.

CLAIRE and ETHAN
CALIFORNIA

Favors to keep

Favors are a fun extra that make a nice gesture to your guests. The best favors are those that are not overly personalized with the couple's name or initials. Think about it: What's your guest really going to do with a frame engraved with your names? To personalize a favor, just add a monogrammed ribbon or gift tag.

When it comes to the actual favor, if your wedding has a theme, then this is the perfect opportunity to give that theme a final push. For example, if you have a fine art theme, a great favor would be small palettes of watercolors. For a literary theme, customized bookmarks in empty journals would be a nice touch. If your wedding doesn't have a theme, it's still nice for the favor to at least tie in to you as a couple. If you love playing puzzles in your spare time, a set of tangrams could be a cute idea. Or if you are tattoo enthusiasts, a set of temporary tattoos is a painless way to share that love. Just remember that favors don't have to be expensive to be memorable. If your guests are able to look at the favor and remember your wedding, then it has done its job!

Creating a welcome bag with a tote customized to the wedding locale is a thoughtful gift, and makes a great souvenir of their trip as well. Since chances are that these guests won't be familiar with the area, you'll want to fill the bag with things to make their stay a little easier, such as maps, an itinerary of the wedding weekend, snacks, and bottled water. The welcome bag isn't required if your budget doesn't allow for it, but it's a nice thought for those who traveled to celebrate your wedding with you.

OPPOSITE: Custom tea towels printed with your wedding date or a design you love are a great keepsake, especially if you make them typographically interesting. The names on the towel are minimal, making the numbers the highlight of the design.

Favors can range from the sophisticated to the quirky, so have fun selecting something your guests will recognize as distinctly you. Personalized totes, buttons, pencils, temporary tattoos, soaps . . . you have so many options!

DIY Keepsake box

Your wedding will leave you with so many mementos to cherish. Why not save them in a keepsake box that you've decorated yourself? The house shape is not only symbolic of your two lives coming together as one, but it is also cute enough to keep out for display! You can paint the house however you'd like, but if you'd like to replicate our design, here's how.

WHAT YOU'LL NEED

- Newspaper (enough to cover your work surface)
- 1 roll artist's tape
- Acrylic or craft paints in 3 colors of your choosing: 2 base colors and an accent color
- One 12-in/30.5-cm square of wax paper
- 2 medium-sized foam brushes
- Papier-mâché house box (available at local craft stores or on Etsy)
- Thin paintbrush
- Package of ½-in/12-mm white vinyl letter decals

1. On the work surface, lay out the newspaper and tape down the edges with artist's tape.
2. Squeeze a bit of each color of paint onto the wax paper.
3. With a foam brush, apply a thin layer of your first base color to the main body of the house. Use even strokes to minimize brush lines. Set the house aside to dry for 15 minutes.
4. In the meantime, take the second foam brush and apply the second base color to the roof of the house, again using long, even strokes. Set aside the roof to dry for 15 minutes.
5. When both pieces are dry, apply a second coat of each color to each piece and then allow to dry for another 15 minutes.
6. Repeat steps 3 to 5 for the insides of both the lid and the box.
7. Now you're ready to add your designs. Using the thin paintbrush, pick up a bit of your accent color and start making thin stripes along the base of the house. It's okay if the lines are not perfect; this will actually give it a watercolor effect. Continue all the way around the house until you get the effect you desire. Set aside the base to dry for 15 minutes.
8. Add any personalization. We used small white decal letters on the roof, but this could easily be painted on as well. You could include your wedding date, location, or a funny inside joke.
9. Allow everything to dry completely and then fill your box with little mementos from the day!

TIPS

- Keeping the paint in thin layers will minimize bubbling on the papier-mâché surface.
- Try a decoupage project. Cover the house with pieces of your favorite paper scraps or photos from your wedding. Even snippets from your wedding vows can create an interesting pattern and texture. Then seal the box with two coats of Mod Podge.

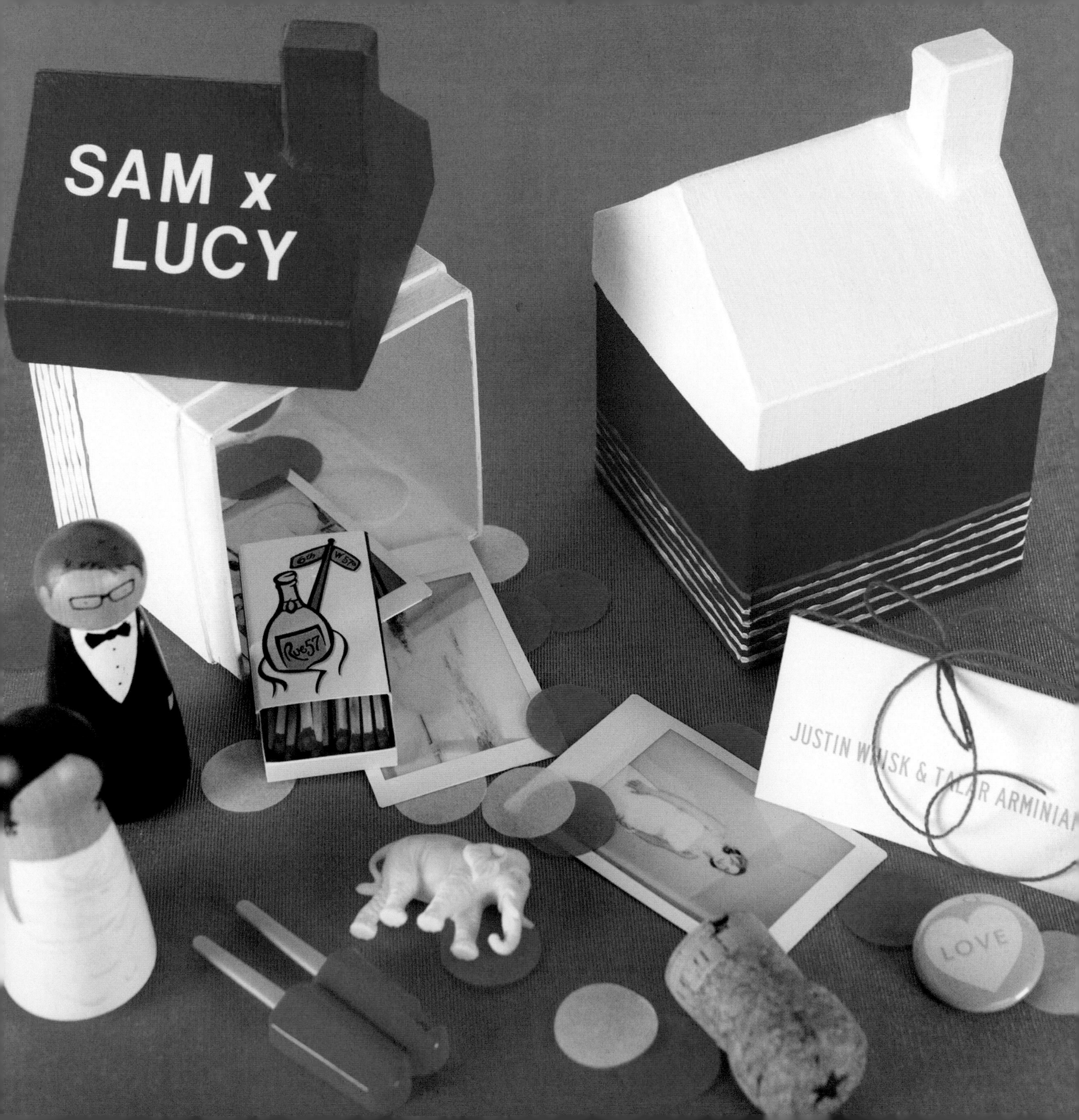
SAM x
LUCY
Rue57
LOVE

PAPER

Ask the expert

MINHEE CHO OF PAPER+CUP DESIGN

Yes, it's true—Minhee is one of the authors of this book. But she's also the creative force behind Paper+Cup Design, the New York–based stationery and design company she founded with her husband, Truman Cho. Since launching in 2003, they have been acclaimed for their work in the design industry in numerous publications such as *Domino, InStyle, Lucky, Martha Stewart Weddings, The New York Times, New York Wedding, Print,* and *Real Simple.* As the creative director, Minhee continues to be a trailblazer in the wedding industry, contributing her modern approach to timeless design.

Q: How does stationery design play a role in the overall design of a wedding?
A: The invitation not only sets the mood and tone for your guests, it is also a guide to how you design your wedding day. From menus, programs, table numbers, and escort cards, having a design theme that can carry through all the paper items will bring cohesion and that extra finishing touch to your overall look.

Q: Why are day-of paper items important?
A: The day-of items are the things that your guests will be surrounded by all through the wedding event, from ceremony to reception. Guests may wish to save their escort cards, wedding programs, and, of course, favors. Think of the experience and memories you would like to give your guests. They also help keep the day running smoothly. Items like programs let guests know what is happening for the ceremony and can lead them into plans for the reception.

Q: What are your thoughts on having a themed wedding?
A: Having a theme to your wedding will keep you from getting sidetracked and help the overall look stay cohesive. But if taken overboard, it will feel too matchy and possibly tongue-in-cheek. The goal is to make the theme look effortless and like a natural extension of a couple's personality. It doesn't have to be overly complex or personal. Something as simple as colors, patterns, or shapes can be enough of a theme to pull together a beautiful event.

Q: What is a polite way to handle online RSVP requests and wedding websites on the stationery?
A: I always prefer a handwritten note but I can see the convenience of an email or online reply as well. I suggest leaving websites off the main invitation. Instead of the traditional RSVP card and envelope, print a small extra insert with the online RSVP request (which will be either an email address or the wedding website). A business card size is great because it can be easily tacked onto a board or refrigerator door.

Q: What are some key qualities to look for in a stationer?

A: First and foremost, a design sensibility that matches your taste. Before booking your stationer, make a list of the things you absolutely need and another list of your wishes. Walk them through your entire vision for the event—décor, food, flowers, and even what you plan on wearing. This will help them understand your priorities and aesthetic. When meeting with the stationer, there are a few key things to ask: What can they do other than invitations and paper? Can they go beyond paper and help with design and décor? If so, can they work with your planner and designer if you have one? The perfect stationer will not only understand your overall vision and help make it into a reality, they will know how to keep a schedule, meet deadlines, and work within your budget.

Q: Any stationery advice?

A: If you go with mailing labels, I suggest printing doubles. Save the second printing for your thank-you cards and have them ready to go as soon as the invites are mailed out. This will save you time, headaches, and stress when the gifts start coming in.

Q: Quick fire: Online save-the-date notice versus printed piece?

A: Printed! Emails get lost and forgotten too easily.

Q: Quick fire: Place cards or open seating?

A: Open seating. Let guests get to know new people. Provide some activities on the table such as conversation starters to help get things going.

Q: Quick fire: RSVP card or postcard response?

A: RSVP card. Leave room for guests to write you a personal note.

Q: Quick fire: Traditional versus nontraditional?

A: Non! Even formal weddings can have some fun thrown in.

Q: Any great color combos you want to see more of in weddings?

A: Using a single color in different shades and textures. This is a simple and elegant look I'd like to see more often!

Q: If you were a color, what color would you be?

A: I love to work with bright colors, but personally I love black for myself.

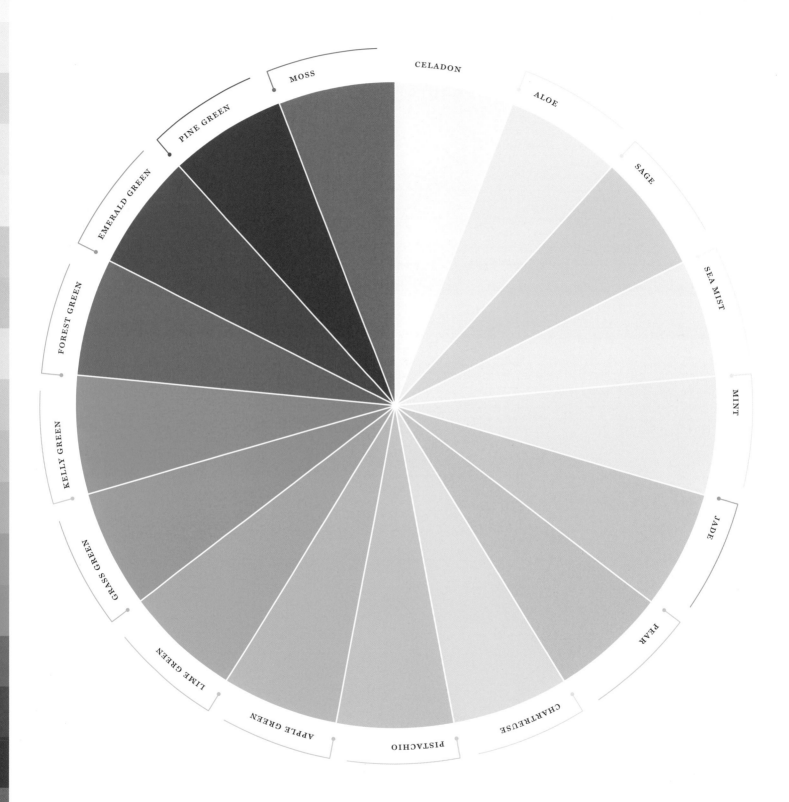

CELADON

ALOE

SAGE

SEA MIST

MINT

JADE

PEAR

CHARTREUSE

PISTACHIO

APPLE GREEN

LIME GREEN

GRASS GREEN

KELLY GREEN

FOREST GREEN

EMERALD GREEN

PINE GREEN

MOSS

Palette

Green looks great in any season because of its abundance in nature. In its grassy and mint shades, green is fresh and happy—even a little playful—but when you start going darker into the olives and emeralds, it is decidedly more formal. No matter the season, you'll see green in almost every wedding—just think of all of the stems and foliage surrounding flowers. Green is symbolic of rebirth and harmony and is very calming (something to remember when wedding planning starts to get stressful!). Green works in any environment and with any level of formality. It is a lovely companion to a whole slew of other colors including but not limited to blue, pink, yellow, and orange. You might not want to pair it with red unless you're planning a holiday-themed wedding.

Centerpieces

You can find dozens of ways to make centerpieces more interesting than the standard flowers artfully arranged in a glass vase. Seasonality of your blooms as well as cost will play a big role in deciding on your centerpieces, but you will see options at every price point.

A general rule of thumb for centerpieces is that you don't want to obstruct anyone's view or their ability to talk to one another across the table. This means either keeping the centerpieces low and out of your guests' line of vision or raising them up above eye level. Generally, centerpieces should either be lower than 12 inches/30.5 centimeters or taller than 24 inches/61 centimeters. Keep in mind the ceiling heights of your venue—lower centerpieces will work better with lower ceilings and taller centerpieces will look better with higher ceilings. Also consider how many pieces of tableware will be part of each table setting. Once you've added the various plates, three types of stemware, serving pieces, etc., there may not be a ton of room left for an oversized centerpiece, especially when seating eight to ten people at each table. For a round table, you can opt for a couple of smaller centerpieces at different heights for a little variation, or one central centerpiece. When seating at a rectangular table, you'll want to place centerpieces at several points down the length of the table, or go with a garland that covers the entire length. If your budget doesn't allow for large centerpieces or yours just look a little small for the table, you can always add decorative elements such as candles, confetti, or even a mirror underneath to magnify the size of the piece.

OPPOSITE: By using grass as the base for this centerpiece, you really get the effect of bringing the outdoors in.

When it comes to the centerpieces themselves, no rule says that they have to be made with flowers at all! If you choose to include flowers, here are some things to consider:

- Don't choose flowers that are overly fragrant. It could drive your allergy-prone guests crazy; plus, when the scent mixes with food, it may not make for a pleasant combination.
- When sticking with a singular color palette, make sure that you have some variation in hue and scale or else your arrangements are going to look dull and not very vibrant for pictures. Since we're focusing on greens in this chapter, look at flowers and foliage in varying shades like grass green, chartreuse, and darker hunter greens.

Forget the flowers! Ferns and foliage are a modern alternative to the standard centerpiece.

Fruits and vegetables are an unexpected element in floral arrangements, but when used on their own, make a stunning display.

- If you want to do something more unique, try arrangements made solely with leaves and foliage, or create terrariums with succulents (they'll last longer than traditional flowers and can become favors for your guests!). You could even do arrangements with beautiful bowls filled with interesting-looking fruits and vegetables such as artichokes, tomatillos, or limes—a modern take on the bounty of nature that can be easily sourced from the grocery store or farmers' market. Best of all, they can all be donated to a local soup kitchen after the wedding.
- If your guests don't take the floral centerpieces home, services in many areas will pick them up after the reception and take them to hospitals or assisted living homes to brighten someone's day.

A striped or patterned fabric wrapped around your vessels will make any plain container look customized.

For something long-lasting that your guests can take home, terrariums make unique centerpieces.

Bridesmaids' dresses

Picking a bridesmaids' dress can be a stressful experience not just for the bridesmaids but also for the bride. Every bride would love to think she's picked a dress that her maids will be able to wear after the wedding, but this is rarely the case. Also, it's not very often that one style of dress will look good on every body type, which is worth taking into consideration when selecting dresses for your bridal party. Thankfully, gone are the days when bridesmaids have to be identical to one another, and you will now find tons of options for every body shape and size.

Before you even begin to look at dresses, settle on the formality of your wedding. If you're going the traditional route where bridesmaids match and "formal" means a long gown and "informal" means a short or cocktail-length dress, then by all means do what makes you happy. However, we're big proponents of not really following the rules, since at the end of day, it's your wedding! Letting your bridesmaids choose their own dresses will make them feel more comfortable since they know what looks good on their body type; it gives them a little more control regarding the cost of the dress as well. To tie all the different dresses together, settle on a unified color palette and allow them to choose within it. You'll end up with a beautiful range of shades and a happy bridal party!

If you'd like a little more uniformity with the dresses, another route is to work with a dress designer that carries a few different styles but in the same fabric. It's a similar idea to letting the girls pick their own silhouette, but instead, your color palette will be even throughout. Companies like Dessy, Donna Morgan, and J. Crew all have multiple dress designs within a certain fabric, so you'll easily be able to find something for everyone.

Bridesmaids' dresses can come in all different lengths, colors, and patterns. Mixing a few makes for an eclectic look!

1

2

3

Guest books

Guest books can be so much more than simply a record of your guests' signatures. They're a wonderful memento of all the guests who came to share your day, and a nice way to collect their well wishes so you can enjoy them again and again. Two things to consider when coming up with unique guest books: 1) how do you plan on displaying your guest book after the wedding (if at all)? and 2) how does it fit into your wedding theme? If, after the wedding, your guest book is going to sit on a bookshelf untouched, then stick with a traditional book format. This can be something as simple as a blank sketchbook that your guests can personalize with mini envelopes, stamps, stickers, washi tape, or even photos. For something a little more interesting, make a stack of postcards that can be mailed to you after the wedding. These can then be stored in a keepsake box. For something more display worthy, take a cheap globe (or you might even get a vintage one off eBay) and paint it to match your wedding décor. Have guests sign it with permanent markers or paint pens and let them go to town with their creativity! This will not only look great at the wedding, but it will stand out afterward in your home.

1: For a guest book that's a bit more compact, set out mini envelopes and notecards for your guests to leave their words of wisdom and tuck them into a scrapbook. **2:** If you're a world traveler or if many of your guests are coming from out of town, a globe makes a fun guestbook that you'll want to keep out on display. **3:** Let your guests get creative with custom stamps, markers, and tape to personalize a traditional guest book with notes and doodles.

OPPOSITE: Have your guests sign postcards in lieu of a traditional guest book and then ask a good friend to mail a few to you every week. It's guaranteed to keep that wedding high going long after the honeymoon!

SEND US A NOTE!
HAPPY 1 WEEK ANNIVERSARY!
MAIL
BON MARIAGE
WE LOVE YOU GUYS!
FOR THE HAPPY COUPLE
SPECIAL DELIVERY
POSTCARD
TO THE HAPPY COUPLE
HAD SO MUCH FUN!
HOW IS MARRIED LIFE?
FOR THE NEWLYWEDS

Cake toppers & serving accessories

Cake toppers and other cake accessories are the cutest way to dress up any wedding cake. You'll find endless options for accessorizing your cake, and the fun part is that you don't have to use a traditional "cake topper." We've seen brides use everything from Lego characters to salt and pepper shakers. The most meaningful toppers are the ones that represent your interests as a couple. For example, if you love to fish, have two fish kissing on top of your cake. If you're typography lovers, a giant ampersand or your initials done in your favorite font are good options. For artists, you can even have something you painted on a mini canvas on a tiny easel. If you're not a topper type, fresh flowers are a beautiful addition and a nice way to tie the cake to your centerpieces or bouquet.

If you're planning on keeping your topper as a keepsake after the wedding, be sure to get some sort of container to keep it in, such as a clear Lucite box or a beautiful glass cloche, so it stays in pristine condition.

Moving our way down the cake, the cake stand and cake knives are other opportunities to bring in some color and fun. Chances are that your wedding venue will have a standard silver or white cake stand for you to use, but if you're willing to spend a little extra money, consider buying your own. That way you'll have a say in how it looks, and you'll get to take it home afterward. The same goes for your cake cutter—instead of borrowing from the venue, it's nice to use one you can keep throughout the years and pass down to later generations.

OPPOSITE: A plain white wedding cake gets jazzed up with colorful accessories such as this fun cake topper, paper flowers, and cake stand.

Nothing is more elegant than jewels. These candy emeralds are a tasty twist on a topper.

Garlands look adorable in miniature.

If you're looking for something more personalized, have silhouettes made in your likeness to top your cake.

A sugar crown in the palest of mints makes a beautifully elegant topper.

WE GOT
HITCHED

Even your cake knife and server can be colorful!

Add a hint of color by adding a bit of ribbon.

This bride and groom (dressed just like the real couple) are adorable, and you'll definitely want to keep them long after the wedding.

Multiple stands in different shades of the same color make a great display for various cakes and desserts.

Signage

Signage is nice to have, but it is not absolutely necessary in all occasions. If you're getting married at a smallish venue where you're the only wedding, chances are you can get away with not having directional signs. However, if you plan on getting hitched in a field of flowers or at a sprawling estate, you might want signs to help your guests find the ceremony location easily. Signage doesn't have to be practical; it can be something completely extraneous that looks nice and adds to the overall décor of your wedding. Decorating the backs of the couple's chairs with "Mr. & Mrs." signs or hanging a sweet pair of portraits are some ideas for lovely decorations that can be repurposed in the home. Food signage is important if you're planning on having a buffet or want to let guests know what's available at cocktail hour, and these can tie into your overall design and color scheme. If you're starting off with a fairly bare venue, oversized signage can even double as a backdrop or fun photo-shoot area. As you work with your florist and/or event planner, they'll be able to recommend areas where signage might be appropriate and enhance the venue.

OPPOSITE: This oversized sign makes a great backdrop for your ceremony or for a photo booth.

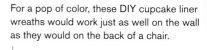

A text garland is an easy and inexpensive décor element that can be used anywhere from the ceremony to the reception.

For a pop of color, these DIY cupcake liner wreaths would work just as well on the wall as they would on the back of a chair.

Don't forget to have signage for any displayed food; your guests will want to know what they're eating!

Oversized X's and O's look cute hanging around the ceremony or propped up as a backdrop when you get married.

Turn an easy piece of art into a memorable display with a few blank canvases, vinyl letter decals, and lots of paint.

Mint "Mr. & Mrs." signs leave no room for wondering whose chairs these are!

Having a custom monogram printed onto fabric for a sign or flag is the ultimate wedding keepsake. Done in a small size, they can line the path that your guests walk along at an outdoor wedding or hang off a rod as a lovely backdrop indoors.

DIY Pom-pom-wrapped bouquet

The fun thing about pom-poms is that once you learn how to use the pom-pom maker, you'll want to make pom-poms for everything! They're particularly nice wrapped around bouquets, hanging off chairs, scattered down the aisle, and anywhere else that could use a little colorful ball of fun.

WHAT YOU'LL NEED

- 3 pom-pom makers in extra large, large, and medium sizes (These are available at craft stores; Clover is the most common brand.)
- Skeins of yarn in various shades of green and white (or any color of your choosing)
- Sharp scissors
- Bouquet already wrapped with floral tape and base ribbon (if using the pom-poms for your bouquet)
- Florist pins

1. Following the instructions on the pom-pom maker, pull open the colored C-shaped arms and start wrapping the yarn around tightly on one side until it looks full and then cut the strand. You'll know when you're about done when the inner curve of the piece disappears under the yarn and it's a snug fit when the arm is closed. Tuck the loose piece of yarn underneath and close the arm. Repeat on the other side.

2. While holding the pom-pom maker tightly shut, use scissors to cut along the center seam on both sides. Take a piece of yarn 10 to 12 in/ 25 to 30.5 cm long and tie a tight knot around the center seam of the pom-pom maker, leaving the tail intact.

3. Carefully pull apart the pom-pom maker and start shaping the pom-pom with your scissors. Make sure to leave the tail alone; you'll use it to hang the finished pom-pom. Continue trimming the pom-pom until you get an even, spherical shape.

4. Once you've made a few pom-poms in varying sizes, wrap the tails of the poms around the base of your bouquet and secure with florist pins. Make sure to leave enough slack so the pom-poms dangle. Or just let your florist take over!

POM-POM VARIATIONS

- For a half-half pom-pom, use one color for one side and another color for the other side.
- For an allover mixed pom-pom, take two different-colored yarns and wrap at the same time on both sides of the pom-pom maker.
- For a large dot pom-pom, wrap one color 20 to 25 times around just the center part of the arm on both sides. Then take your other color and wrap it over the center and around the rest of the arm. Once you cut and shape the pom-pom, you should have a circle within the pom-pom.

FLOWERS *Ask the expert*

SARAH BRYSK COHEN OF BLOSSOM AND BRANCH

Sarah Brysk Cohen has worked in flower shops across the United States for twenty years. Always eager to explore new ideas and express her cutting-edge, distinctive approach to floral design, she opened the Blossom and Branch studio in Brooklyn, New York, in 2009. She's also a regular columnist and resident floral expert for various online publications.

Q: Why is it important to pick seasonal flowers?

A: Choosing seasonal flowers is of utmost importance for optimal quality and pricing. If you are someone who has dreamed your whole life (or through the life of your pinboard!) about holding lily of the valley in your bouquet or having peonies bursting forth from centerpieces, it is worth considering a wedding date based on the season in which these flowers are in bloom. It is a totally legitimate option to decide that you want a spring wedding, for example, because you love the look and feel of the flowers available during that time. It might also say something larger about your taste or the feelings evoked during that particular season, which in turn will guide the rest of your décor and planning. Your florist really and truly wants you to be happy, so if you give them a little flexibility by saying, "I love the look or color of Flower X. Can you either get that for me in this season or select another, similar bloom that might work for me?", they will try their best to accommodate your wishes.

Q: What flowers are not ideal for weddings?

A: Generally speaking, flowers that are fragile or weak without hydration or can't stand up to tough conditions aren't the best choices. Wedding flowers, particularly bouquets, have to endure a lot during the course of a wedding—transport, photography, sitting out in heat or cold. Many times, clients have asked me for a particular bloom for a corsage or boutonniere, and I come up with an alternative that I know is more durable. Also, flowers that are highly allergenic (such as fragrant lilies) can be risky, as you might run into trouble with a reaction from guests. The best florists don't just say "Yes" if your requests are tricky; they use their expertise to guide you to the optimal seasonal blooms.

Q: What are some ways to get a color that isn't readily available in nature?

A: I love to integrate whimsical touches into weddings, so I might be inclined to select an organic element, such as foliage or some variety of pod, and actually paint it with special floral spray paint. Aside from painting, the most straightforward solution is to select vessels, candles, or other decorative items to be included on the tables in your color of choice. Clients often bring me a paint swatch or a Pantone color and ask that I find a way to work it into their décor, even if it is not through an actual bloom.

Q: Why are flowers for weddings so expensive?

A: Wedding flowers are expensive for several reasons:

1) Flowers themselves are expensive, even at wholesale prices. This is because flowers are temperamental, difficult to grow, difficult to ship (even "local" flowers are almost never grown proximal to flower markets), and there are many people who need to get paid to make flowers grow and sell. I always say that there are hundreds of hands that touch the flowers before I pull them out of a bucket at the flower market. And if you are working with quality materials, the price is that much higher. Even with less-expensive individual blooms (say, carnations) there is a big visual and experiential difference between a fresh, quality bloom and one that is not as high caliber.

2) Once the flowers are purchased, there is a lot that goes into getting those flowers designed and delivered to the wedding such as conditioning the stems, transportation, installation, and cleanup. Expenses of space, salaries, and insurances also add to the individual stem costs.

3) Variance in florist pricing can be explained by several factors, and there is value in hiring someone a bit more expensive if that means securing a more experienced florist. Experience makes the difference when it comes to the myriad crises that can arise during the planning and execution of a wedding. Most of these crises happen behind the scenes and an experienced florist ensures that you never even have to know that anything went amiss. Remember: you are also paying for at least one person's time for the year, six months, etc., leading up to your wedding when you are working to develop the scheme for your big day. All that expertise and time (every phone call, email, etc.) is folded into the cost of your wedding flowers.

Q: What are some ways to work around a tight floral budget?

A: The very best way to work around a tight budget is to let your florist be your guide. Some of my favorite clients are the ones who have limited budgets and only give general parameters. They might say, "We love this particular palette or this particular look. Can you design a wedding within our budget around this?" The fewer specifics you require in a situation like this, the more freedom your florist has to bring blooms or ideas you might never have considered and to give you the most bang for your buck. Trust your florist! I never shy away from taking on a modest-budget wedding where I have almost total design freedom. I can always come up with something wonderful—it's my job! Any specific suggestions for saving money (aside from working with seasonal blooms, perhaps substituting candles for fresh flowers in some areas) relate to your particular season, theme, venue, and so on, which is why it's best to consult your florist.

Q: Quick fire: Pastel or punchy?

A: Punchy! I love saturated color, and it photographs well.

Q: Quick fire: Indoor or outdoor?

A: Outdoor! I love an outdoor ceremony and an indoor reception. You get to experience the natural light and beauty of your venue (and hopefully a gorgeous day) and then move into a more formal atmosphere for the evening.

Q: Quick fire: Mix or match vessels?

A: Mix! My favorite look is an eclectic mix of elements. This can look very shabby chic or surprisingly elegant, depending on the vessels.

Q: If you were a color, what color would you be?

A: Orange. I have always loved the color orange, and in florals, it comes in a wide spectrum, from dusty peaches to bright corals to dark pumpkin tones. And my personality tends toward the bright and sassy, so orange seems to fit.

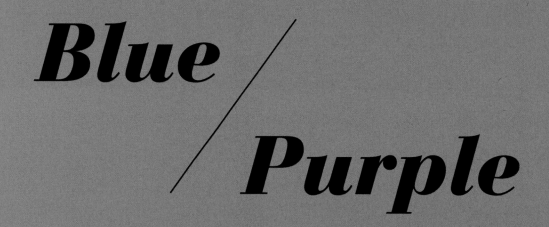

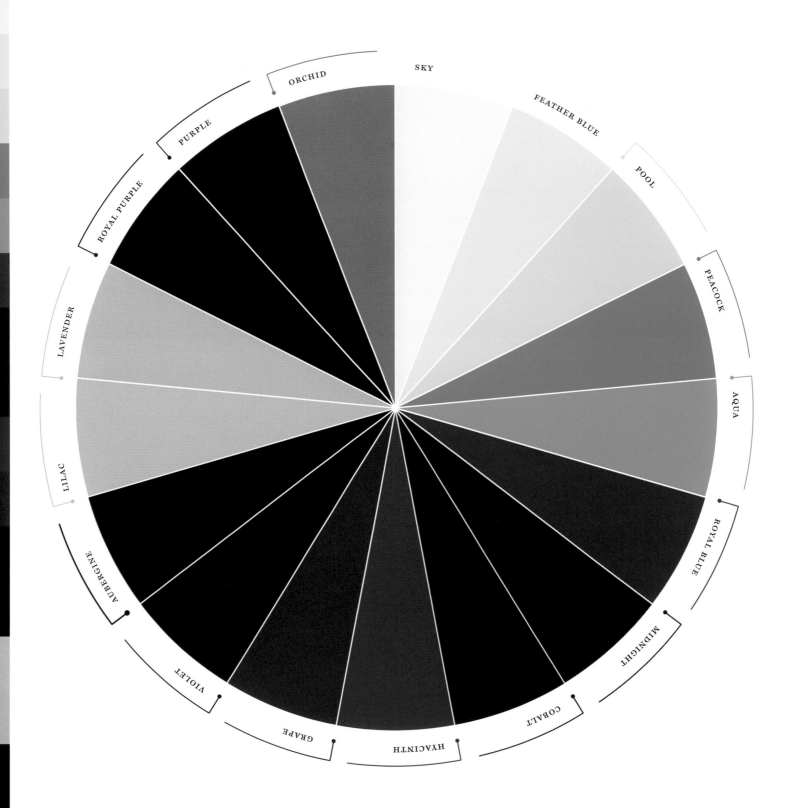

Palette

Blue is a magical color that, no matter the color palette, always manages to find its way into a wedding (something borrowed, something blue, anyone?). It's one of those colors that can change the emotion it evokes with its shade. Pale icy blues are soft and romantic; navy blues feel more classic or nautical; and turquoise reminds us of the beach. Seasonally, it works better for the summer or spring months, or even winter in its icier form, but not quite as well for autumn. That's not to say you couldn't use it, but with so many other autumnal colors to choose from, it might be hard to find a place for blue.

Purple is very similar to blue in that its feeling changes with its shade. But purple has a deep history rooted in royalty, which gives it a more noble presence. It's a popular color for outdoor or garden-inspired weddings in its lighter forms of lavender and lilac (it doesn't hurt that so many flowers come in these shades, either!). In its darker shades, purple is a wonderful base for a formal or urban-set wedding. Purple can skew warm or cool, depending on how much red or blue is in it, so it can play nicely with colors from both sides of the spectrum. Our favorite play with purple is to layer multiple shades (light, medium, dark) for a richer tonality.

Boutonnieres

Though they are small, boutonnieres pack a real punch when it comes to adding color to the groom's and groomsmen's attire. We love it when all the boutonnieres are within the same color family, but each is designed a little bit differently. The groom's boutonniere should definitely stand out, whether by size or by a contrasting or complementary color. It's nice if the boutonnieres correspond with the bridal party bouquets, but if not, white is always a safe bet. If your groom isn't feeling the whole flower thing, boutonnieres can be made out of a number of supplies, from herbs to twigs to cotton or even small toys and buttons. If your guy isn't into boutonnieres at all, they can be nixed altogether in favor of a pocket square. Just be sure the groom feels good in whatever you choose.

OPPOSITE: No rule says that boutonnieres have to be made solely of flowers. Here we've got a mix of real and fake elements such as fabric and paper flowers, wired fabric leaves, spotted feathers and twigs, and even scrapbook embellishments.

Shoes

Shoes are often a place where brides take a little more liberty with color. Given the old saying "something borrowed, something blue," it's not uncommon to see a bride with blue shoes! Luckily a white dress goes with every color, so whether you choose a full-on colored shoe, simply a touch of color on the sole, or a shoe clip, it will work with the outfit. If you can't bring yourself to go with colorful shoes for the ceremony, remember that you can (and probably will want to) bring a pair of flats in a fun color for the party afterward.

If your bridesmaids are all in the same dress, it's fun to give them free rein when it comes to their shoes. By sticking to the same hue, they will stay looking cohesive but still be able to show off a little personality.

Gentlemen of the bridal party have plenty of opportunities to sport some color in their footwear, too, from laces to colored soles, to patterned socks, to—if they're more daring—a colorful shoe. For casual weddings, we've seen more than our fair share of grooms and groomsmen wearing Converse sneakers in multicolored hues. More high-end designers are coming out with dress shoes in fun colors, too. These can be a refreshing change from the serious black dress shoe.

OPPOSITE: A little pop of color from beneath your wedding dress can definitely count as your "something blue"!

What better way to show your
excitement than with a DIY
"YAY" shoe clip or shoe insert?

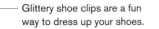

Glittery shoe clips are a fun way to dress up your shoes.

If blue shoes aren't your thing, purple is a great substitute.

A light lavender pair of pumps gives a subtle hint of color under your dress.

Grooms and groomsmen can get in on the action with colored laces and soles.

9.9.15

K+M

So many ways to accessorize . . . the possibilities are endless!

PAPER

Calligraphy

Calligraphy adds a wonderful contrast to ultra-modern printed invitations, especially when done by incredibly talented calligraphers like the ones shown here. Each has his or her own particular style unique to the traditional Spencerian script; it's hard to pick a favorite! When starting your search for a calligrapher, the best place to begin is online. Check out magazine and blog vendor listings or peruse Pinterest and set aside a bunch of calligraphers' work you like. One nice thing about calligraphy is that you don't necessarily need to use a local person—you can send envelopes to them to work on while you start prepping your invitations. Once you've selected a couple of potential vendors, ask them to send you samples of their work so you can see it in person. Also get an idea of their per-envelope costs. Calligraphy pricing is generally between $2 and $5 an envelope, but it could be higher depending on the calligrapher. Most calligraphers have different styles, from adding girly flourishes to staying very linear. When picking a style, be aware of legibility. You don't want your invitation to get lost because the postmaster couldn't read the address.

Envelopes aren't the only place to showcase this age-old craft. If you have the budget, your calligrapher can do your escort cards, favor tags, overall signage for your wedding, or even a decorative marriage certificate. If budget is an issue, you can ask them to write out "Thank You" or your names and have the words turned into a stamp to use on other paper goods. Another cost-cutting solution is to download a calligraphy font that you can print and trace yourself.

OPPOSITE: As you can see, calligraphy can take all sorts of forms. Styles range from whimsical and quirky to straightforward and minimal. Some can include flourishes; others can take up the whole envelope. Try out different calligraphers to see who will mesh the best with your invitation design.

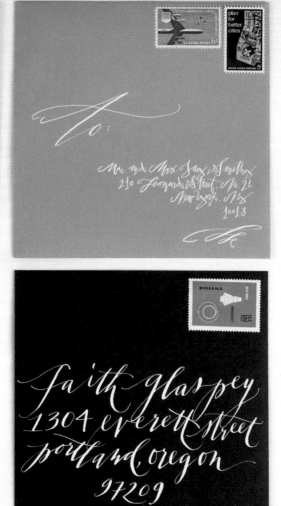

Signature cocktails & accoutrements

Signature cocktails are a great way to add personality and color to the bar for your guests. Come up with a single cocktail that represents you *and* your fiancé or have a cocktail named after each of you individually in corresponding colors. You can work with the catering company or bartender for the event to come up with ideas or just come up with something on your own. Even if liquor isn't made in the colorway you're looking for, you can use syrups or fruit purées to bring in the special color. (If you're having a signature cocktail for your guests, don't expect it to take the place of the entire bar . . . you're still going to need basics like beer and wine to even it out.)

If the color of your wedding doesn't lend itself to a drink, you can always work color in with drink accessories: straws and drink stirrers (better for taller glasses, unless you cut them down) and napkins, coasters, and garnishes. You can also add color with fruit or ice cubes!

OPPOSITE: Signature drinks are a wonderful way to personalize your wedding. Include your favorite drink, your fiancé's favorite drink, and one you both love or that screams "let's celebrate!" like champagne. Keep the look cohesive by using elements of the same color for each, from garnishes to rims to accessories.

his   ours   hers

SIGNATURE COCKTAIL COLOR IDEAS

BLACK: blackberries, coffee. *Cocktails*: Black Russian, Cuba Libre, Espresso Martini.

BLUE: Alizé Bleu sparkling wine, blueberries, Blue curaçao, Hpnotiq.
Cocktails: Berrytini, Blue Hawaiian.

GRAY: not the most appetizing of colors, so we suggest sticking with Grey Goose vodka or gray accessories. *Cocktails*: Early Grey Fizz, Grey Lady.

GREEN: cucumber, green apples, honeydew melon, kiwi, limes, mint leaves, rosemary, thyme. *Cocktails*: Apple Martini, Mint Julep, Mojito.

METALLIC: this color is a bit harder to work with since nothing edible in nature is metallic looking, but that's the beauty of ideas like edible gold and rimming sugars. *Cocktails*: Gold Rush, Silver Fizz.

Colorful reuseable ice cubes will cool down a cocktail without watering it down. Colored rock candy can flavor warm drinks.

Straws and stirrers are probably the easiest way to liven up a drink (other than the alcohol!). When they're patterned or customized for the occasion, they even double as favors.

ORANGE: kumquat, orange, peach, tangerine.

Cocktails: Mimosas, Peach Sangria, Tequila Sunrise.

RED/PINK: strawberries, cranberries, grapefruit, grenadine, raspberries, red currants, rose petals, triple sec, watermelon.

Cocktails: Bloody Mary, Pink Panther, Strawberry Daiquiri.

VIOLET: crème de violette, edible violets, elderflower, grapes, lavender.

Cocktails: Gin Cassis, Purple Rain.

WHITE: coconut, cotton candy, crème de cacao, ginger, lychees, white rum.

Cocktails: Lychee Martini, Piña Colada, Pisco Sour, White Russian.

YELLOW: lemons, mango, passion fruit, pineapple. *Cocktails*: Ginger Lemonade, Lemon Drop.

Napkins and coasters can be customized with your initials, your wedding date, or even funny sayings.

Rimming sugar comes flavored or plain, so you can find a color to coordinate with any signature cocktail you dream up.

Napkins can be foil printed with a small graphic as a dainty detail.

STYLING Garlands

With the rise in social media at weddings, having Instagram-worthy backdrops has become an important part of the décor. Garlands are a simple but impactful way to create backdrops for you and your guests to make memorable photos for your wedding. Not only are they easy to source, but they are incredibly easy to make, even without a sewing machine.

The possibilities are endless when it comes to making a garland. You can go as simple as the old grade-school standard of linking paper rings or make little washi tape flags, to more complex ideas like ombré-dying fabric strips and sewing them together. We've seen garlands made of vintage stamps, felt, photos, fabric, paper, letters, sequins, ribbon . . . if you can string it, chances are you can make it into a garland! Depending on how much time you have, you may or may not want to tackle this yourself. Luckily that's what bridal parties (and Etsy) are for!

Garlands don't have to be limited to backdrop duty at your wedding. You could make a tiny version to use as a cake topper, use them to line the aisle at your ceremony, drape them behind the altar, or place them artfully over your dessert table. Clustering a bunch together in different shades of the same color is fun in a messy way, but arranging them neatly is just as good. There's no wrong way to display a colorful garland!

OPPOSITE: A photo booth backdrop doesn't need much to be successful. Here, we hung colored paper painted with a simple frame and draped it with a garland. Color-coordinated photo booth accessories tie it all together!

ABOVE: You have so many varieties of garlands to pick from, from buntings to tassels to fringe!

Chocolate décor DIY

Adding your own chocolate lettering or other chocolate decorative element is a fun
way to dress up and personalize a dessert. If you don't want to tackle this for your actual wedding,
try it for a bridal shower or a bachelorette party. Make the letters and designs ahead of time and
keep them in the fridge until you're ready to decorate your cake or treats.

WHAT YOU'LL NEED

- Chocolate lettering template
  (www.chroniclebooks.com/weddingsincolor)
- Printer paper
- Baking sheet
- Wax paper—enough to cover your work surface
- 8 oz/225 g colored chocolate discs (You can find
  these online or in baking stores.)

- Microwave-safe bowl
- Decorator tips in varying sizes
- Cake decorating bag or large plastic bag with
  one corner snipped
- Flat spatula

1. Download the chocolate lettering templates you wish to use and print onto regular printer paper. (It doesn't matter what kind of paper, since it will go underneath the wax paper.) Place the printed templates on the baking sheet and top with the wax paper.

2. Place the chocolate discs in the microwave-safe bowl and microwave for 30 seconds. Stir the chips and microwave in 30-second increments until the chips are nearly melted. Remove the bowl from the microwave and continue stirring until the chips are fully melted.

3. Attach your desired decorating tip to the cake-decorating bag. Fill the decorating bag with the melted chocolate (be careful; it will be hot!) and, with a steady hand, start tracing the template designs onto the wax paper. (Practice a few letters off to the side until you get used to the flow.) Lines that are too thin will break when you take them off the paper, so keep lines medium-thick and consistent while drawing.

4. Once you've finished drawing your letters and designs, stick the baking sheet uncovered in the fridge or freezer so the chocolate can harden. It should take only half an hour or less to really get

hard enough to work with, but the longer it can stay in there, the better. Unless you've got a completely empty fridge or freezer, you won't want to make these too far ahead because they take up a good amount of space.

5. Once the designs have hardened, use the flat spatula to remove the chocolate pieces from the wax paper and arrange them on your dessert or plate before serving. It's so easy that soon you'll be making these for all your desserts!

TIPS

- Make the letters in small batches; it's easy for your hand to cramp up if you're not used to working with the decorating bag. The chocolate will also start to harden in the decorating bag, so start with a little bit at first.
- If your lines are too thin, you can go over them again to add thickness and dimension.
- For specific chocolate colors that aren't readily available, you can make your own by combining white chocolate and food coloring. However, you'll have to use an oil-based or powder-based food coloring to color it. Regular food coloring won't work and will just ruin the chocolate.
- You may want to have a towel on hand to hold the pastry bag when you're piping because it will be hot at first.

Ask the expert

XOCHITL GONZALEZ OF A.A.B. CREATES

Xochitl (so-cheel) Gonzalez founded A.a.B. Creates (formerly called Always a Bridesmaid) in 2003 with fellow Brown alumna Mayra Castillo after cutting their teeth producing the international CLIO Awards. Using niche marketing, media savvy, and social media, they have grown their organization into one of the country's most sought-after design and planning firms for clients seeking creative, out-of-the-box wedding experiences with understated luxury. Their global client roster is a who's who in the worlds of entertainment, finance, tech, and fashion. In 2010, the ladies formed a new company, called Just About Married, that offers one service only: "day-of" coordination. In 2006, they launched their award-winning blog AlwaysaBlogsmaid.com. Additionally, Xochitl is the wedding expert for About.com and has served as a contributor to RealSimple.com and the *Huffington Post*.

Q: What are the benefits of hiring a wedding planner?
A: A planner is a great way to streamline your ideas for your wedding and to make the most of your budget. A great planner knows which elements and details will enhance your wedding and which will be a waste of money. With so many fabulous ideas and products out there, it's helpful to have someone knowledgeable on board to help you edit down your options. They can make sure you don't overpay for things and can help prioritize costs. A planner will also help with time management, especially for couples who are busy with work or planning a wedding in a town far from where they live. A wedding planner can essentially keep your wedding moving forward while you are busy leading your life.

Q: What's the difference between a wedding planner, an event designer, and a "day-of" planner?
A: Typically, a wedding planner works with couples from engagement until the wedding day, assisting them in finding a location, finding great vendors, negotiating contracts, coordinating hotel blocks, and arranging transportation, as well as managing the day of the wedding itself.

A day-of planner, on the other hand, manages the execution of plans you have already put in place. They come in about a month before the event to make sure that you've dotted all your i's and crossed all your t's and then reach out to your vendors to find out their load-in and load-out times. Most day-of planners will do things like set up the escort cards, set out favors, cue toasts, and help with any family photos, among other things. You should think of them more as event managers who can troubleshoot any unforeseen problems rather than planners.

Finally, an event designer focuses on the look and feel of your wedding—not just flowers and tabletop, but the aesthetic of the whole space. Many wedding planners are also event designers, but not necessarily. An event designer will help you create a fantastic floor plan, have ideas for lighting and décor, and help conceive of little details like favors, table numbers, menu cards, food stations, and welcome bags. They are not involved in logistics of the day—just designing and installing the aesthetic elements.

Q: About how much does it cost to hire a planner?
A: I'd say you are looking at anywhere from $2,000 to $5,000 for month-of coordination and $10,000 and up for full-on planning!

Q: What are the key things to look for when selecting a planner? How do we find the right planner for our needs?
A: Finding the right planner is similar to finding the right future spouse: a great planner for one person is not necessarily a great planner for someone else! The first thing to do is assess your key concerns about the wedding. Is it that you're getting married in a remote location and you're worried about transportation and logistics? Is it that you want it to be stunning and possibly featured on a blog and need someone to manage all the pretty details? Are you concerned about food and food service? Identifying your biggest concerns allows you to shop around for planners with the most expertise in that particular area. Of course, the type of planner you need changes how you assess candidates as well. If you need a day-of coordinator, look for someone who seems kind but firm, organized but also flexible, experienced but not bossy. If you are looking for a full-service planner, find someone you like. You will be spending a lot of time with this person! If you are looking for an event designer, be sure that you love his or her aesthetic, that they have the ability to generate unique ideas, and that they listen to your vision. I think it's important to interview at least two planners. Asking friends for referrals is always a good idea. There is nothing like hearing about firsthand experience with someone's work to make you feel more at ease about hiring them.

Q: What is one thing a wedding can do without or *can't* do without?
A: I've never seen anyone regret the money spent on photography: the eye of your photographer shapes the way you remember your own wedding day. Similarly, don't scrimp on catering or cut things like waiters or bartenders: your guests won't notice that you added in $1,000 of flowers on the table, but they will notice if they have to wait for a drink. If you have out-of-town guests, don't skimp on the welcome gift at the hotels, but *do* feel free to forgo a favor. Generally speaking, favors are wonderful but not necessary. It's better to put the money into details that directly impact your guests.

Q: Quick fire: Band versus DJ?
A: DJ with live music for the ceremony.

Q: Quick fire: Garter toss or skip it?
A: Skip it!

Q: Quick fire: See each other before or after?
A: BEFORE! Sure, it's romantic for him to see you at the ceremony for the first time, but it's more romantic to have a nice quiet bit of time to see each other and take photos together before the big moment.

Q: Quick fire: Sweetheart table or sit with the bridal party?
A: Sweetheart table!

Q: If you were a color, what color would you be?
A: I'd be green. It's the color of both forests and jewels.

White

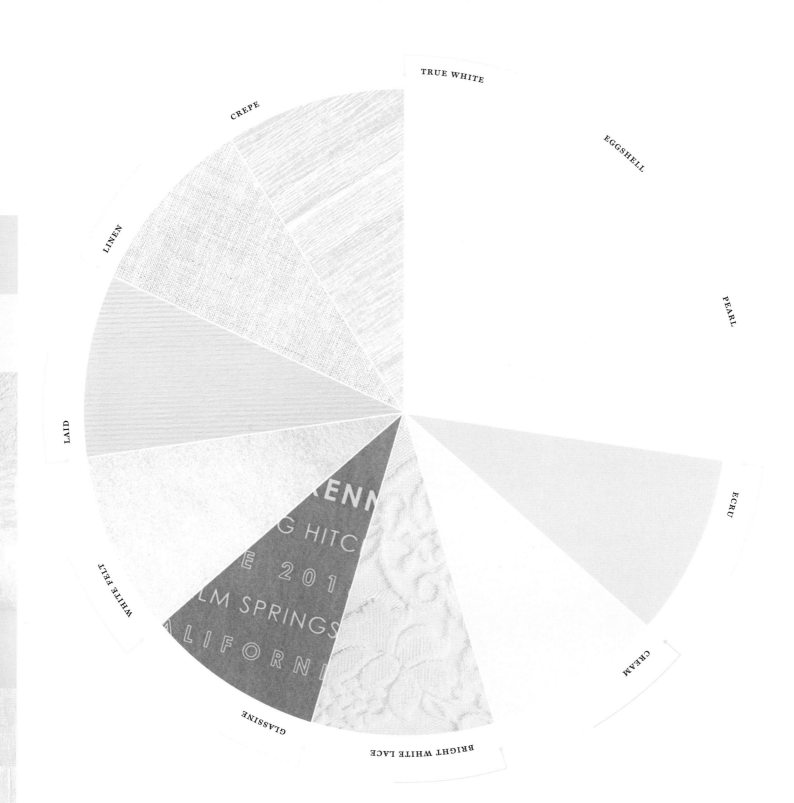

TRUE WHITE

EGGSHELL

PEARL

ECRU

CREAM

BRIGHT WHITE LACE

GLASSINE

WHITE FELT

LAID

LINEN

CREPE

Palette

As you plan your wedding, chances are that white is going to play a big part. (Unless you decide to go with a colored wedding dress!) White is the perfect blank slate and, symbolically, a representation of your new beginning as a married couple. But open up any paint chip deck, and you'll discover there's no *one* white . . . there are dozens of whites! Add a bit of yellow or brown to white, and you've got ivory; add a hint of blue, and you've got an icy undertone; and add red to take it a tad warmer. Under certain types of light or even outdoors, white can drastically change shades. Because of this, when meeting with vendors or heading out to source for your wedding, it's imperative to take swatches with you (no matter what color you're working with) so you can see how the different shades work together. When working with white, try to stick with two shades at the most; use any more than this and you risk having your palette look like a mistake. Once you have your whites selected, start playing with textures. An all-white wedding can look dull if there's nothing exciting happening with the details. Ruffles, lace, and sequins are all elements to consider when working with white. Differences in sheen and translucency will help break up the monotony of the single color. An all-white wedding has the potential to be amazing; just make sure you include some variety to keep it interesting.

Floral headpieces

FLOWERS

For brides who may not necessarily want to do a veil but still want to do something special with their hair, a floral headpiece is a terrific option. A large headpiece, a single flower behind your ear, or a dainty floral crown are all beautiful options and can work with practically any hairstyle. If you're planning on wearing your headpiece only for the actual wedding, then by all means, go for real flowers. They are beautiful but will eventually start to wilt, of course. For something with more longevity to last the night, fabric, paper, or even patent leather flowers are the better option. Bring inspiration images to your hairstylist to discuss your options and keep your eyes open for interesting hairpieces. Bridal salons will almost always have hairpiece options to show you, too.

While this headpiece of real flowers takes some guts to wear, it makes a stunning statement piece for a modern wedding, indoors or out.

A simple crown of posies is perfect for an outdoor garden wedding with a flowing dress.

We took our inspiration from the runways and styled these hairpins in a lovely cascade.

This delicate fabric floral comb goes particularly well with a low chignon.

These silk oversized orchids with just the slightest bit of veiling are a super-chic detail for any style of wedding.

Wedding dresses

A bride will agonize about few decisions more than she'll agonize about her dress. It is one of the most important outfits you'll ever buy, and since all eyes will be on you, of course, you want to look like the best version of yourself! When searching for dresses, the best place to start is magazines and blogs. As you pull dresses that catch your eye, think about your body shape and which silhouette will accentuate your best features. If you're tall, you'll want to stick with simpler silhouettes with little embellishment; if you're short, stay away from anything oversized such as voluminous skirts, because you'll just get lost in them. Your venue will also help dictate the dress style; a beach wedding requires a very different dress from one in an urban loft or city hall.

Once you've pulled some images and settled on a venue, it's time to start trying on some dresses! Starting six to nine months ahead of your actual date leaves enough time for the dress to get made (they are generally made to order) and for alterations. If you already have a veil, accessories, shoes, or undergarments, bring those to your appointment so you can see how they look with the dress, along with one or two trusted friends who can give you honest opinions. Don't get discouraged if some of the dresses that looked great on the magazine page don't look the same on you. There is a perfect dress for everyone out there; you just have to keep trying! Often a dress style you never thought would work ends up being the surprise winner.

Wedding dresses and accessories normally eat up about 10 to 15 percent of the wedding budget and, if especially elaborate, maybe more. But if money is tight, have no fear; you still have options! Every wedding salon out there has sample sales and trunk shows that sell designer dresses at discount. Buying off the rack is another option, especially if time is of the essence, and lots of ready-to-wear companies have started bridal lines. Chances are you'll still have alterations to deal with, but the overall cost will be a lot less than with a dress from a salon. Bottom line is that you want to feel comfortable and beautiful in whatever dress you pick, so take your time, try different styles, and enjoy the process.

DRESS SILHOUETTES

- Ball gown
- A-line
- Mermaid (also known as Trumpet or Fit and Flare)
- Column (also known as Sheath)
- Empire waist
- Tea-length (also known as Cocktail-length)
- Mini

NECKLINES

- Sweetheart
- V-neck
- Asymmetrical
- Off the shoulder
- Halter
- High neck
- Bateau
- Illusion
- Scoop
- Strapless
- Cowl
- Queen Anne

NEXT SPREAD: We've covered all sorts of necklines, hues, and price points with these wedding dresses, and each and every one is a stunner. Note how many different shades white can come in! Try on a few different types to find the one that's best for your skin tone.

Save-the-dates

While save-the-date notices aren't a critical part of your wedding invitation suite, they are absolutely necessary if you're planning a destination or holiday-weekend wedding. You want to give your guests ample time to plan or save money so they can attend and, especially, to mark off the date in case another wedding comes along. Generally you want to send your save-the-date six to nine months before your wedding. If you've created a B-list guest list (a list of people you are still unsure about inviting), do not send these people a save-the-date since then you'll be obligated to send them an invitation as well. Information you'll definitely want to include on the save-the-date are your names, the wedding date, the wedding location (not necessarily the venue if it hasn't been locked down yet), and a wedding website if you plan to have one.

Some experts disagree on whether or not the save-the-date should match the invitation in design or formality, but we like to think of it as a chance to do something really fun, especially if the invitation itself is going to be formal. Save-the-dates are a great way to get your guests excited, so play up the location or theme of the wedding! If you're getting married at a beach location, maybe you'll want to send a small bottle of sand with the save-the-date attached; for a camp-themed wedding, a small box with a toy compass inside would be fun. It can even be as simple as a "Greetings from . . ." postcard. This is your chance to do something memorable.

OPPOSITE: With monochromatic designs, you've got to be creative to keep them interesting to the eye. Laser cutting and blind embossing are two ways to get good readability, and so is changing up the hues of your color, in this case, whites to ivories. Adding little elements such as a leather tag or felt adds juxtaposition to the smoothness of the paper. The translucent version is simply a white design silk-screened onto vellum paper.

SAVE THE DATE

Shayna & Noe

6/4/16

IXTAPA MEXICO

SPECIAL ANNOUNCEMENT

Jessica & Mark ARE GETTING MARRIED!

JUNE 2016 • SAN FRANCISCO

SAVE THE DATE

THERESA & SAM

ARE TYING THE KNOT!

MAY 21ST 2016

CHARLESTON, SC

www.theresaandsam.com

HARRIET + KENNETH

ARE GETTING HITCHED!

JUNE 2016

PALM SPRINGS

CALIFORNIA

♥

INVITE TO FOLLOW

Dessert bar ^{FOOD}

Dessert bars can either complement the wedding cake if you're having one, or if not, can take the place of it entirely. It's all about the display, and it's the perfect opportunity to work in some of your favorite desserts. If you don't have the time to do it yourself, you can seek out the expertise of your caterer or baker or else find a dessert-bar specialist who will take care of every little detail.

If you want to tackle creating a dessert bar yourself, it is definitely doable. It's just a matter of finding stands at varying heights and plates that all work well together. Working with a singular color palette guarantees that all the elements will work together seamlessly, and incorporating some varying shades will keep it from looking dull. Start thinking about desserts that you'd like to include. They'll be sitting out for a while, so don't pick anything that needs to stay cold unless someone is there to serve or replenish. Cupcakes, cookies, and donuts are always crowd favorites, but you can work in candies, truffles, mini milk-shakes . . . pretty much anything your heart desires. Play with heights and levels using cake stands, clear boxes, or even plates resting on vases so that the display doesn't look flat. You can even work in little details like toppers to some of the desserts for added interest. Depending on the size of your table, you have the ability to double up on identical desserts at opposite ends so that people can access it from both sides. Six to eight different types of dessert should be a good starting point. Have some signage describing what's being offered and provide glassine bags or small take-home boxes so that your guests can load up for the ride home. It's definitely a sweet way to end the evening!

OPPOSITE: Signage is a great design element to pay attention to when designing your dessert bar. It makes everything look more festive.

Mini donuts in a variety of
toppings are always a crowd
favorite.

Anything in miniature is an
automatic hit with guests.

Leaving out some boxes with the
desserts lets them become a great
takeaway favor.

Plain marshmallows get the
special treatment when dipped
in chocolate and sprinkles.

Fondant engagement ring toppers
are a sweet way to bring a wedding
theme to dessert.

OPPOSITE: A color-themed dessert bar is the ultimate
way to serve a variety of desserts to your guests in a
stunning display.

Table numbers

Table numbers are one of those details that can be overlooked or treated as an afterthought, but are actually a great opportunity to incorporate your wedding theme into the reception. It's also a detail that can be totally fun, quirky, and easily DIY'd! One thing to keep in mind is that table numbers should be easily visible to your guests so that they have no trouble finding their table; make sure the number displays work with the height of your center-pieces. For taller centerpieces, stick with a smaller table number; do the opposite for small centerpieces. The number could even be worked into the centerpiece itself. When it comes to the design of the actual number, get creative. You could cut up old photographs, attach house numbers to books, display toys brandishing numbers signs, or even have alarm clocks set to the right "time" on each table!

OPPOSITE: Think outside the box when it comes to table numbers. Anything from a child's toy robot to an alarm clock can be transformed into a unique display piece.

DIY Embellished vases

If you're looking for a way to dress up a plain glass vase, this is probably the easiest DIY idea you'll find. And your guests will be fighting each other to take them home!

WHAT YOU'LL NEED

- Newspaper (enough to cover your work surface)
- Glass cylinder vases in varying sizes (These can be found in craft or floral design shops.)
- Glass cleaner
- Paper towels
- 1 box of pop-up glue dots
- Glue gun with extra glue sticks
- Spray paint (We used Montana Gold in matte and glossy finishes.)

1. Lay out a couple of sheets of newspaper to protect your work surface. Plug in the glue gun, allowing time for it to heat.
2. Using the glass cleaner and paper towels, wipe any dirt or fingerprints from the vases.
3. For the large polka-dot vase, arrange glue dots in a decorative pattern on the vase's surface. We arranged ours with a lot near the top of the vase and tapered the dots toward the bottom. The glue dots are malleable and sticky, so remove them from their packaging as carefully as possible to maintain their shape and avoid touching them too much once you have placed them on the vase. When you've finished your design, set the vase aside.
4. For the small lines of dots, get out the glue gun and, starting from the top, apply small glue dots in a line around the vase. It's okay if the gun leaves a trail of glue leading to the next dot; it actually adds to the pattern! We went about three-quarters of the way down the vase in our example. When you've completed your design, set aside the vase and allow the dots to dry.
5. Move outside or to a well-ventilated area for spraying. Lay out more newspaper and apply two coats of spray paint to the entire vase in whatever color you choose. Allow time for the paint to dry between coats.
6. Voilà! Unique vessels for your centerpieces!

TIPS

- Experiment with different patterns so that each vase is unique.
- For a more intricate pattern, print out a design you like, tape it to the inside of the vase, and trace over it with the glue gun before spray painting on the finish.

DRESSES *Ask the expert*

GABRIELLA RISATTI OF GABRIELLA NEW YORK BRIDAL SALON

Prior to opening her bridal boutique in 2008, Gabriella Risatti spent a decade working in the buying offices of world-renowned fashion labels including Ralph Lauren and Calvin Klein. Her experience and knowledge of the fashion industry coupled with her desire to create a unique and personalized shopping experience for brides led to the opening of Gabriella New York. Since then, Gabriella has quickly been recognized as an expert in the bridal industry. At Gabriella New York, the belief is that shopping for a wedding gown should be memorable, personal, and genuinely enjoyable.

Q: What should brides look for when selecting a wedding dress?
A: She should take into account her personal style, the venue, her body type, and the formality of the wedding. Once all of this has been considered and she has tried on enough gowns, she has to listen to the way she feels in the gown. A bride will feel beautiful and happy when she puts on the right dress. Most importantly, she cannot be easily influenced by others. If she loves the gown, it doesn't matter what anyone else thinks!

Q: How soon should brides start shopping around for a dress?
A: Wedding gowns purchased from bridal salons are all made to order, meaning that each gown is made especially for each bride. For this reason, it does take time! I recommend women purchase their gown eight months before their wedding. This gives the designer four months to make their gown and our seamstress four months to complete the alterations process. As a rule of thumb, I recommend two months of shopping time before construction or alterations start so the bride has plenty of time to look around. Brides with shorter engagements that don't allow for a custom dress to be made can definitely look to off-the-rack options, where alterations will have a much shorter lead time.

Q: How should a bride decide what kind of veil goes with what style dress?
A: Things to take into consideration when selecting a veil are the venue, the style of the gown, the fabric of the gown, and the overall vibe of the wedding. If a bride is getting married in a church or synagogue, for example, a long, cathedral-length veil is not only appropriate, but also stunning! On the other hand, if the venue is outside near the beach, I recommend a shorter veil, such as an elbow-length or fingertip veil, so that it doesn't get tangled when the wind blows. I also like to consider the seam lines of the gown. For example, if the bride is wearing a gown with a natural waist, I recommend selecting a veil that either goes to the waist or the hem of the gown. This way, the veil doesn't create another line. Overall, the veil should be an accent to the gown and should never take the attention away from the bride's face or gown. If a bride is wearing a full lace gown, I recommend pairing it with a veil that has a lace

border, which begins around the shoulder rather than at the comb so that the lace doesn't distract from the bride's face. If a bride selects a gown that has a lot of detail such as beading or embroidery, I generally recommend a simple veil with a pencil edge. A very detailed veil can be too much when paired with a very detailed gown. For a simple satin or charmeuse gown, I love the look of a silk-trimmed veil. It has a way of framing the bride in a very elegant way.

Q: Is there a dress that flatters all body types?

A: I think that finding some silhouette that works for all is a tough challenge; however, the A-line silhouette is as close to this as possible. The A-line is a great universally flattering style because, as the name implies, the skirt is an "A" shape, which hides the hip area very nicely without adding volume. A seam at the waist is often a nice addition because it draws the eye to the smallest part of a woman's body.

Q: What are some ways to add color to a standard white wedding dress?

A: Accessories! I wore vintage lavender earrings on my wedding day, and I loved having that little splash of color. We also see a lot of women wear a sash on their gown in another color such as champagne, blush, or even blue. Many brides wait until the reception to put on the sash in order to signify they are ready for the party!

Q: Is gown preservation necessary after the wedding? How do you feel about "trash the dress" sessions?

A: If you want to keep your wedding gown for potential future use, gown preservation is absolutely crucial. If you don't, your gown will yellow and possibly deteriorate over time. Even if you don't think you'll ever have a daughter who would want to wear your gown, I encourage brides to save their gown because you really never know. I had my mom's wedding dress shortened and altered and wore it to my bridal shower. I did

the same with my (now) mother-in-law's dress and wore it to the family dinner the Thursday night before our wedding. It was incredibly special and sentimental and made them both so happy!

I dislike the "trash the dress" trend because, even if you don't want your wedding gown, rather than ruin it, there are many, many women out there who can't afford a proper wedding gown. Donating it to a charity, such as Brides for a Cause, is a much better way to get rid of it!

Q: Quick fire: Matching or mismatched bridesmaids' dresses?

A: Matching.

Q: Quick fire: Veil or no veil?

A: Veil! (When else do you get to wear one!?)

Q: Quick fire: Garters—dated or a timeless tradition?

A: Dated.

Q: Quick fire: White or colored wedding dress?

A: White.

Q: If you were a color, what color would you be?

A: Lavender. Not only do I love the way this color looks, I also love all the different varieties of the lavender plant. Lavender is appealing to almost everyone and also goes with a large variety of colors. Because it is originally part of nature, it doesn't look out of place in our homes or on our bodies.

LADURÉE
Paris

Eleanor Sofia
and
Elliot John

CORD ALLY INVITE YOU
TO CELEBRATE THEIR LOVE

ON SATURDAY, THE 14TH OF JUNE
TWO THOUSAND AND FOURTEEN
AT SIX O'CLOCK IN THE EVENING

THE LITTLE CHAPEL
Atlanta, Georgia

DINNER & DANCING TO FOLLOW

Encre Noir

LOVE

Mrs. Kristen Armstrong
2321 SOUTH NEWSTEAD AVENUE
SAINT LOUIS, MISSOURI
6·3·1·0·5

THE RETURN
ELL·O PUDDIN' POP
AY - SEPTEMBER 23RD
7PM UNTIL U CAN'T EAT ANYMORE
87 STUYVESANT
TIME TO GET S
ICE

LOVE IS SWEET!
MELISSA AND MATTHEW

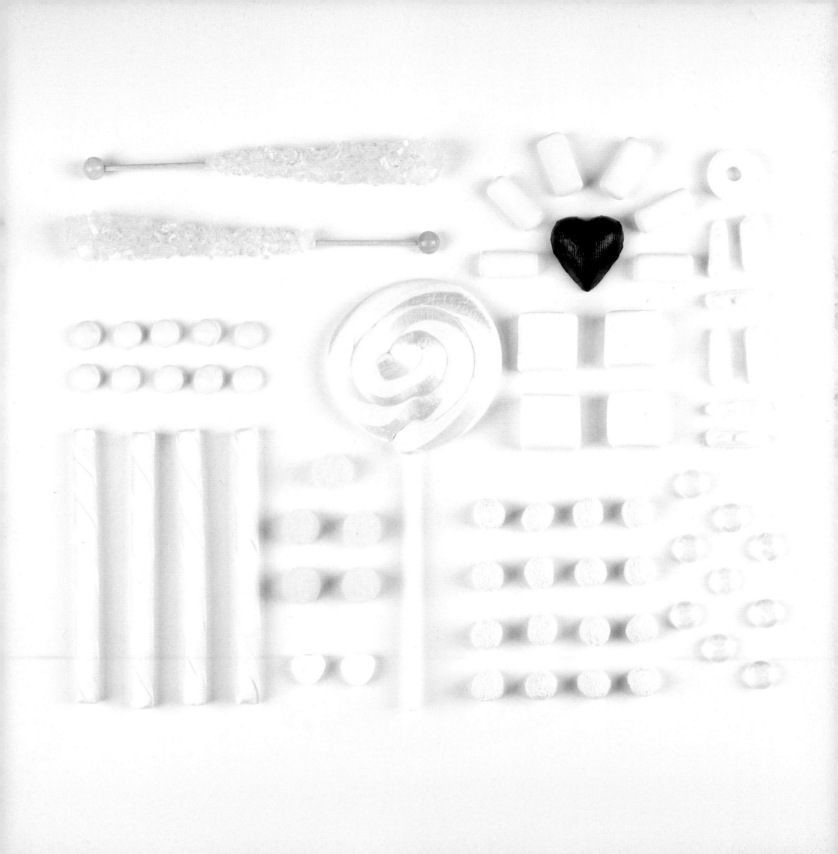

Palette

When you think of a black-and-white wedding, what do you picture? If you envisioned a glitzy, black-tie affair, you'd be in the majority. But that doesn't mean the palette can't work just as well in a less-formal setting such as a restaurant, or even outdoors. The nice thing with black and white is that the combination works for every season and every type of occasion.

If you're working with a color combination as simple as black and white, the trick is to add interest in the details, such as patterns. It's important to pay attention to scale, because pairing too many large patterns can be overwhelming. As a general rule of thumb, sticking with an odd number of patterns is best—three is a good starting point. When considering scale, start with a large pattern as your main focus and then pair it with complementary patterns of smaller scales. As an example, let's take a table setting. The tablecloth can be used as the large pattern, your napkin the smaller pattern, and a textured centerpiece can serve as a medium-sized pattern. Remember that textures count as patterns as well, so don't limit yourself to polka dots and stripes; look at patent leathers, velvets, and vinyls, too. Great places to seek inspiration for patterns are interior design magazines, books, and blogs. Look at living rooms and notice how the rug pattern compares to that of the curtains or the pillows on the sofa. We've included some of our favorite patterns to give you a jumping-off point.

Decorating your bouquet

FLOWERS

In addition to flowers, consider how you'll decorate your bouquet. A black-and-white palette doesn't present too many options for flowers, so the bouquet accessories are a great way to create something unforgettable. Traditionally, the stems of bouquets are wrapped with lengths of ribbon neatly tucked and folded, but why not have a little fun? Instead of one ribbon, have a bunch cascading down the bouquet in different patterns and textures. The ribbons will look great in photos and add a playful element to your bouquet.

Or maybe you want to try something a little more daring. After all, how many times in your life do you get to carry a bouquet, anyway? Tassels from the ribbon store add a whimsical yet sophisticated element to a bouquet. Pom-poms are easy to make with a pom-pom maker from the craft store. (Check out our easy DIY project in the Green chapter!) Bring in colors that aren't typically found in nature by painting silk flowers or leaves.

Generally your florist can take care of all this for you, but you'll want to have a discussion with them about logistics and thoughts about what you want to use. Chances are they've done something similar and can give you advice about how it will work.

OPPOSITE: An otherwise white bouquet gets the royal treatment with a cascade of beautifully patterned black-and-white ribbons.

Tassels, which can be easily sourced online or at a craft store, make for a delicate decoration.

Take some leftover personalized ribbon from your favor packaging and wrap it around your bouquet.

Oversized pom-poms are a unique and fun way to accessorize.

A favorite handkerchief or scrap of special vintage fabric added to a bouquet brings meaning and adds charm.

A locket can be a nice way to remember a beloved family member or friend on your special day.

Groom & groomsmen

Men have certainly come a long way from the days of ill-fitting tux rentals, and many are choosing to take a more active role in selecting outfits for their weddings. Thanks to more and more bespoke tailors cropping up around the country, more and more men are having their suits or tuxedos custom-made. When deciding whether to opt for a suit or a tux, the groom should consider the formality of the event as well as the season. If you want the classically dapper James Bond look, a black tuxedo is the obvious choice (with navy as a possible exception). Anything else, and he risks looking dated in photos (remember *Dumb and Dumber*?). For suits, blacks, grays, and blues are classics, but you have room to play with fabric choice. Seersucker is perfect for a summer wedding on the beach, while thicker fabrics such as wool or felt are better for winter. Since the color of the suit itself will be relatively conservative, it is good to accessorize with color. Patterned socks and novelty cufflinks are an understated way to bring in some personality, and he can bring in some more color with a pocket square or tie.

No hard-and-fast rule exists when it comes to the groom matching with his groomsmen or his bride. It's always nice when the groom can stand out a little bit. One option is for the groom to wear a bow tie while the groomsmen wear ties, or perhaps the groom wears a suit in a slightly different shade. As for matching with the bride, it's as easy as plucking a flower from her bouquet and using it as a boutonniere or pulling the bridal party's color in with a pocket square. When in doubt, keep it simple! You definitely don't want to over-accessorize, especially when you need only a pop of color to modernize a classic look.

OPPOSITE: Let your inner nerd fly with these adorable eyeglass cufflinks.

OPPOSITE: Sure, not everyone will see your awesome socks unless you sit down, but at least YOU will know they're stylish!

Graphic pocket squares can replace a boutonniere if your groom would prefer to stray from the floral.

Giving each of your groomsmen a different pair of fun socks makes for a great photo op!

A quirky detail on the shirt is a fun, unexpected move.

The ultimate classic in wedding wear for men is the tuxedo. Finishing it off with a patterned pocket square makes this look more modern.

You can't go wrong with a dark suit! Pair it with a patterned shirt and tie to add a bit of life.

Men's dress shoes don't have to be your usual shiny wingtips; the velvet dress slipper is an elegant alternative.

PAPER

Invitations & printing techniques

The invitation sets the tone for the whole wedding. It is how your guests will know when, where, and how your wedding will take place, in addition to giving them a taste of the event's style. If there's any time to stick to tradition, this is it: just because you *can* email your invitation doesn't mean you should!

Your first step is figuring out the ultimate design direction for your invitations. Consider the level of formality: Black tie? Cocktail attire? Casual? For a formal event, you may want to be a bit austere with your invitations, focusing on clean lines and elegant fonts, but for a more casual affair, feel free to go wild with pattern and texture! You'll want the invitation to relate somewhat to the design of your wedding. If you're not using a theme, you can always work in a hint of your wedding colors. The wording of the invitation and even the style in which you address the envelope will also let your guests know the level of the event's formality. We recommend doing a quick online search to find all of the different wording and address variations because you'll find dozens of options. Choose the version that feels best for you.

OPPOSITE: This invitation by Minhee was digitally printed in Futura Standard with white ink on black paper but then duplexed (white paper sandwiched between two pieces of black paper) and beveled (cut on an angle) to elevate its formality. The loose floral illustration and graphic envelope liners keep it playful.

LOUISE BRODERICK
AND
HAYDEN MOORE

REQUEST THE HONOR OF YOUR PRESENCE
AT THEIR WEDDING

SATURDAY, THE TWENTY-FIFTH OF JULY
TWO THOUSAND FIFTEEN

AT HALF PAST FOUR IN THE AFTERNOON

HOTEL ARTS BARCELONA
BARCELONA, SPAIN

RECEPTION TO FOLLOW
BLACK TIE

1

Mr. and Mrs. Wayne Trice
request the honor of your presence
at the marriage of their daughter

Amy Elaine to
John Hunter Hoskins
May 25th 2015

at half past five in the evening

Founders Memorial Garden
University of Georgia
Athens, Georgia

Festivities to follow

2

ELLIN IDRIS TODD
REQUESTS THE PLEASURE OF YOUR COMPANY
AT THE MARRIAGE OF HER DAUGHTER

STEPHANIE MAE
TO
WARREN MICHAEL

SON OF INA KLEIN-LIEBMAN

JULY 18TH, 2015

AT SIX O'CLOCK IN THE EVENING

DEL POSTO
85 TENTH AVENUE
NEW YORK CITY

7

TOGETHER *with their* FAMILIES
Erin Michelle
Crews
AND
Nicolas Jacques
Pirog
REQUEST THE PLEASURE *of your* COMPANY
AT THEIR WEDDING
Saturday, the twelfth of October
two thousand thirteen at six o'clock in the evening
KING PLOW ARTS CENTER
887 WEST MARIETTA STREET NORTHWEST
ATLANTA, GEORGIA
Reception, dinner & dancing
immediately following the ceremony

5

Mr. & Mrs. Paul Armstrong
REQUEST THE PLEASURE OF YOUR COMPANY
AT THE MARRIAGE CEREMONY OF THEIR DAUGHTER

KELLEY
ELIZABETH

&

MICAH
DAVID WILLIAMS

Saturday, August sixteenth, 2014

BEGINNING AT SIX O'CLOCK IN THE EVENING

FENWICK HALL GRAND BALLROOM

RICHMOND, VIRGINIA

3

TOGETHER WITH THEIR FAMILIES

VIOLET QUILL & JAMES CURRANT

REQUEST THE PLEASURE OF
YOUR COMPANY AT THEIR WEDDING

SATURDAY THE SECOND OF MAY, TWO THOUSAND FIFTEEN AT 6:30 PM
VERITAS VINEYARDS | CHARLOTTESVILLE, VA

6

J + A

JENNIFER GREENE & ALISTAIR WALTON BLEVINS
REQUEST THE PLEASURE OF YOUR COMPANY AT THEIR WEDDING
SUNDAY JUNE TWENTY THIRD
TWO THOUSAND FIFTEEN AT ONE-THIRTY IN THE AFTERNOON
BROOKLYN BOTANIC GARDEN

AND AFTERWARD A CHAMPAGNE RECEPTION

4

DR. AND MRS. DAVID THORNDIKE
REQUEST THE HONOUR OF YOUR PRESENCE
AT THE MARRIAGE OF THEIR DAUGHTER

RACHEL PERCY
TO
JACOB EUGENE MEYER

SON OF MR. & MRS. DAVID MEYER

SATURDAY, THE SIXTH OF SEPTEMBER
TWO THOUSAND AND FOURTEEN
AT THREE O'CLOCK IN THE AFTERNOON
GEDNEY FARM
NEW MARLBOROUGH, MASSACHUSETTS

DINNER AND DANCING TO FOLLOW

R J

You don't have to spend a ton of money on invitations to make them impactful. Cost will vary depending on quantity and the printing method you use, as well as the number of pieces in the suite. The most expensive forms of printing are engraving and letterpress, which also tend to be on the formal end, while digital flat printing or printing at home is far more affordable. Costs can also rise when you start adding special details such as foil stamping, edge painting, beveling, or duplexing. How you order your invitations can also have a huge impact on price. It is still common to go to a stationery store and select your invitation from a binder filled with different designs and templates. Alternatively, you can go directly to the designer and have your invitation custom-made. You can also order ready-made designs that are customizable online or even download designs and print your invitations at home. With all of these choices and some time and patience, you can create a formal-looking invitation with a limited budget. If you're looking to save money, skip using an oversized or square invitation because these will always require more postage.

When it comes to how many pieces to include in your invitation suite, there's no right answer. Key pieces you can't leave out are the invitation itself (including important information like the date, time, and place of the ceremony), a separate reception enclosure if the reception is elsewhere, and the RSVP card with a stamped, self-addressed envelope so that your guests can respond. It's always nice to include accommodation information as well as maps and directions, especially if the majority of your guests are coming from out of town. If you're looking to cut costs, a good place to start is with the extra inner envelope or tissue paper you might find in some invitations. When you're ready to place your order, be sure to account for extras because inevitably some invitations will get lost in the mail, but more important, your invitation is a great keepsake. We recommend getting at least ten extra just in case.

Accessorizing your invitations can be a wonderful way to add some personality, especially if the invitation is simple. From adding a pattern to the backing or to the envelope liner, to using whimsical calligraphy to address the envelopes or vintage stamps to add color, it's the little things that will really add to the "wow" factor when your guests receive them.

OPPOSITE:
1: This mix of hand-lettered and digitally printed serif text has a composed yet friendly feel. (Letterpress by Printerette Press)
2: Digital print with whimsical illustrations on front and a square backer. Although the information is black-tie formal, the invitation itself is done in a fun way. (By Mr. Boddington)
3: Custom die-cut with elegant typography. (By MaeMae Paperie)
4: This digital flat-printed invitation uses vector-created floral illustrations that tend to be more modern. The illustration carries over to the backer. (By Thoughtful Day)
5: This interactive die-cut invitation has flaps that open up to reveal the text. (By Cheree Berry Paper)
6: This hybrid mix of die-cut punch and letterpress features a fun envelope liner for a modern twist. (By Egg Press)
7: This invitation was done completely by hand and letterpressed. It's a modern twist on the traditional invitation, done in calligraphy. (By Ladyfingers Letterpress)

Edible favors

Edible favors are a way to give your guests a special taste of your wedding. Tons of options for edible favors exist, including personalized candies, pretzels, cookies, jars of honey, spice seasonings, and more. Think of them as tasty souvenirs and make them personal to you as a couple so that they hold some significance for your guests.

When coming up with ideas for edible favors, think about some of your favorite treats, or a food that's popular in the location of your wedding. Getting married in New York City? Nothing is more New York than a black-and-white cookie, or alternatively, you could do a gorgeous apple with a custom label on it. This would also be a great opportunity to do something handmade, like your grandmother's famous chocolate chip cookies. Offer a sampling of the baked goods with a personal touch like a recipe card explaining their significance to you. Customized candies are also a great way to go and many vendors will personalize lollipops, hard candies, or even M&Ms by putting your picture or initials on them.

Packaging is another opportunity to personalize favors that may come in bulk or need a little help in the aesthetics department. A simple glassine bag can be made all the more special with a customized label or a ribbon printed with your names and wedding date. You can also turn a plain white box into a stylish keepsake. Feel free to look outside of the standard packaging materials to find a unique vessel for your favors; we love glass test tubes and tiny origami candy boxes to add a little whimsy.

Piñatas have been all the rage lately, so making them in a miniature size for dispensing your favors is a unique way to up the fun factor in an otherwise formal affair. We were lucky enough to find these bow-tie versions (opposite) ready-made. We filled them with custom candies, but if you're the ambitious type, you could definitely make these yourself or enlist the help of your friends and family. They're a little time consuming, but by enticing some friends with a bottle of wine, you can make it a fun bonding activity!

OPPOSITE: How adorable are these mini bow-tie piñatas? We filled ours with custom bow-tie and high-heel candies from Papabubble to reflect this wedding's black-tie theme.

Get creative with patterns by dipping pretzels in black-and-white sprinkles.

A LITTLE *something* FOR YOU!

♥

SARAH & JAKE

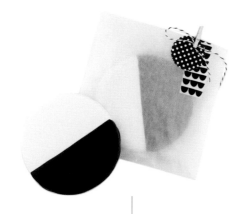

The famous black-and-white cookie doesn't need much to make it shine—just a glassine bag, a little bit of graphic tape, and a ready-made tag clipped on with a tiny clothespin.

A simple cupcake becomes so much more with the addition of a graphic belly band and liner.

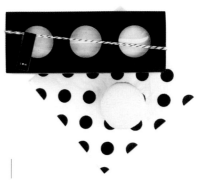

The clear windows of this triple macaron box enable the color to pop through, and a simple initialed tag is the perfect add-on to the black-and-white baker's twine.

Glass test tubes are a chic way to package little chocolate candies.

These origami paper candy boxes hold only a small handful of sweets, but make an adorable keepsake after the candy is gone.

Create a simple yet striking favor by wrapping your favorite chocolate bar in pretty paper. You can also create custom wrappers for added personalization.

Infused oils, honeys, or even vodkas look adorable in miniature form.

STYLING

Ring pillows

Ring pillows are a great opportunity to have a little fun and do something memorable. Traditionally, ring pillows are small cushions holding the couple's rings, carried down the aisle by a younger member of the bridal party. Generally this job is done by a young boy, acting as the counterpart to the flower girl. These days, couples are getting more and more creative with this element of wedding tradition, from using creative alternatives to the standard pillow to having well-behaved pets act as ring bearers.

For those who want to stay with the traditional ring pillow, a great way to modernize it is to use a patterned fabric or to add some decorative trim. But no rule says that a ring pillow has to be white or satin, so hit the fabric store and find something with personality. To make it more of a keepsake, you could use vintage fabric, a swatch of a fabric that holds meaning for you, or custom-made fabric. Once you have the fabric chosen, you can embroider your initials and wedding date or iron your engagement photo onto it.

Conversely, there's no reason that a ring pillow has to be a pillow at all! Consider using a favorite novel or book of poetry to hold your rings. If you feel uneasy about hollowing out a book, simply attach the rings to the top securely with decorative ribbon. Tying a ribbon around an oversized stuffed animal doubles as a gift for your ring bearer and looks adorable coming down the aisle. A small wooden box could be customized with names and dates and could be kept in your home as a jewelry box after the wedding.

One thing to consider when having a child walk down the aisle: you may not want to have the actual wedding rings on the pillow, especially if the child is a little rambunctious! Have the best man slip the actual rings into his pocket for safekeeping and leave a dummy pair on the pillow for show.

1: Nothing says you're excited to get married like having a piñata hold your rings! It's easy enough to make yourself by adding tissue paper fringe to a papier-mâché box, filling it with confetti, and resting your rings on top. The confetti can double as something to toss as you head back down the aisle.
2: How beautiful is this wooden ring box? You can find lots of unique options on Etsy.
3: Using a copy of your favorite book to present the rings is an excellent option for literature-loving couples.

Our favorite alternative to the ring pillow is the idea of "walking" (but really carrying) a balloon dog down the aisle with the rings tied around its neck. Your guests will love it, and it can double as a gift for the ring bearer.

Accordion-style guest book

This DIY project is a guaranteed way to get your guests talking to each other. For a bonus, leave a Polaroid or Instax camera on the table with some washi tape to include funny group shots from your guests! You can view figures 1–3 at www.chroniclebooks.com/weddingsincolor.

WHAT YOU'LL NEED

- Accordion Guest Book templates (www.chroniclebooks.com/weddingsincolor)
- Four 11-by-17-in/28-by-43-cm sheets of white text-weight paper (woven texture results in nicer finishing)—2 for the cover and 2 for the inside panels

- Utility knife
- Self-healing cutting mat
- Metal ruler
- Glue stick or double-stick tape
- Bone folder (optional)
- Two 4-by-6-in/10-by-15-cm sheets of chipboard

1. Download the Accordion Guest Book Interior template and your choice of the Accordion Guest Book Covers template and print each onto an 11-by-17-in/28-by-43-cm sheet of paper. Customize your cover texts prior to printing them. There are several versions to choose from to accommodate small and large table numbers in two different design options.

2. Cut along one side of the vertical trim marks from the panel prints labeled "Interior 2" using the utility knife, cutting mat, and ruler. Cut along the dotted vertical line of the "Interior 1" page. This is the extra margin where glue will be placed.

3. Apply glue to the back edge of the trimmed side of the "Interior 2" page using the glue stick. Place the edge flush against the second panel's crop marks and press the pieces together to create a six-panel accordion.

4. Trim the left and right edges from the crop marks. Gently fold each panel at the fold marks, alternating the direction of the fold to create the gatefold look. Using the bone folder will make the lines crisp. Once all of the panels are folded, trim at the top and bottom crop marks.

5. Cut out the front and back covers about 1 in/2.5 cm from the crop marks. (This will ensure that you have enough bleed area for an overlap when gluing the covers down.)

6. Center the front cover on one of the chipboards by aligning the crop marks to the edge of the board. Flip the chipboard over and tuck in one corner first and then tuck in the adjacent corner of the paper. Apply glue to the top edge of the cover and fold over the paper that is in between the corners. (This will create a clean cornered edge.) Repeat the process for the other three sides. (See Fig. 1.)

7. Repeat step 6 for the back cover. Let both covers dry.

8. Apply glue to the edges of the first panel of the interior pages. Align the edges with the inside of the front cover. Press the interior and front cover together. (See Fig. 2.)

9. Fold in the accordion pages and then apply glue to the edges of the last panel of the interior pages. Align the edges with the inside of the back cover and press the interior and back cover together. Set aside to dry. (See Fig. 3.)

Ask the expert

DANIEL & BRENNA LEWIS OF BROOKLYN TAILORS

Brooklyn Tailors was founded in 2007 when husband-and-wife team Daniel and Brenna Lewis began offering custom fittings out of their Brooklyn apartment. As word spread, they opened their first storefront in Williamsburg, Brooklyn, to the delight of stylish men all over the country. Along with their first store came the launch of their first ready-to-wear shirts, suits, casual pants, and neckties. Their collections are built around the core belief that good design begins with the best materials and construction practices and is rooted in the traditions of classic menswear.

Q: Why go the bespoke route for suits?

A: Bespoke suits are great for a couple of reasons. First, it's an entirely original pattern, so you can perfect the fit for your body, taking into consideration posture and problem areas. The other reason is that you have full control over all of the stylistic details: from lapel style and width to button material and placement and everything in between; so you get exactly what you want. Bespoke isn't always necessary, but it's a great option, especially for those who have trouble fitting well into off-the-rack suits.

Q: When is it appropriate to wear a suit versus a tux?

A: Most occasions only call for a suit. A smart, tailored, well-fitting, classic suit will cover you in nearly every situation except ones that specifically call for black tie. Then you've got to wear the tux.

Q: Do all groomsmen need to match?

A: No. While it's more traditional to have all groomsmen dressed the same, we are seeing an increasing number of grooms who just select a suit color and let their groomsmen choose something that fits their style and budget. If it's a more casual wedding, there really are no rules. I prefer seeing a groomsman comfortable in what he is wearing, rather than stiff in something he didn't pick out. I feel they look best when they get to select what they feel the best in and what reflects their personal style, rather than something rented.

Q: What are some ways to bring in some personality to an otherwise classic look for the groom or groomsmen?

A: Suits are a real investment, so unless you have a big budget to play with, we suggest buying a classic suit in gray or navy and using the shirt, tie, socks, or shoes as places to add a pop of personality. Even a mid-gray wool suit with a classic white dress shirt and a more-interesting tie can have a lot of impact. Be careful with combining too many accents in one outfit. It's best to figure out the item you want people to remember and then keep the rest of the outfit clean and simple. It gives more oomph to the piece, too.

Q: Is it possible to overaccessorize?
A: Absolutely! See above.

Q: Quick fire: Bow tie or tie?
A: Hands-down: tie. I am not a fan of the casual bow tie except on a Southern gentleman.

Q: Quick fire: Two-piece or three-piece suit?
A: Two-piece. It takes a very specific person to pull off a three-piece without looking stuffy or overdressed. A two-piece is always a safe bet.

Q: Quick fire: Downtown or uptown?
A: Downtown.

Q: Quick fire: Sneaker or dress shoe?
A: Dress shoe, especially with a suit. There are great ways to make a suit seem more casual, but sneakers are not my favorite option.

Q: If you were a color, what color would you be?
A: The cobalt blue of our store awning. It's classic but a little more interesting than you'd expect.

Todd L
Jacqui Lee
Andrea Cho
Calli Pucci
Perla Cost
Lucia Costa
Anna Sui

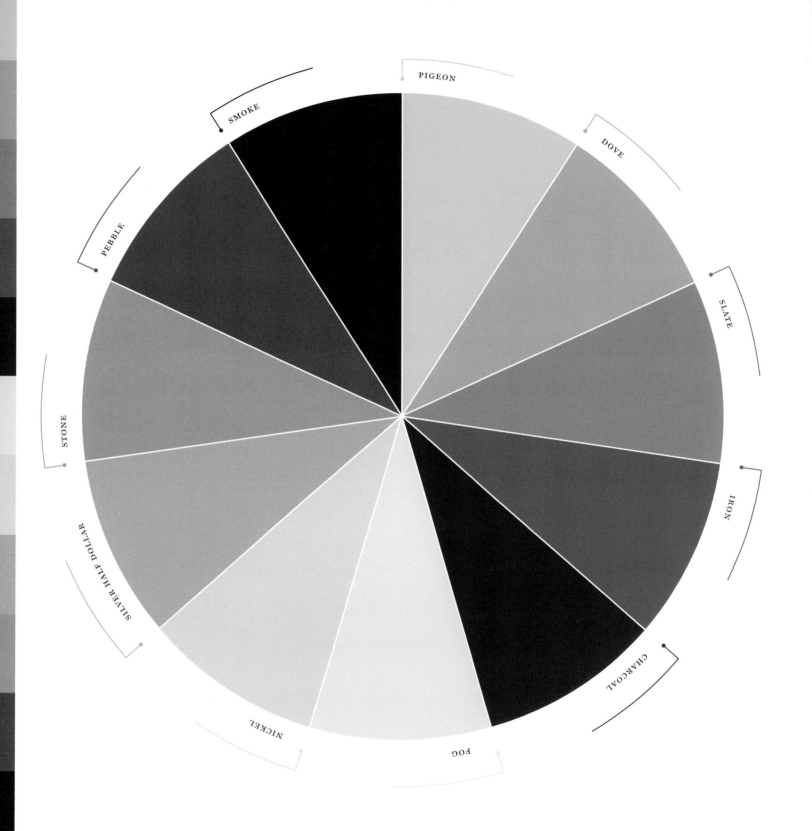

PIGEON

DOVE

SLATE

IRON

CHARCOAL

FOG

NICKEL

SILVER HALF DOLLAR

STONE

PEBBLE

SMOKE

Palette

Gray is a sophisticated and sleek color. It's no surprise that it is gaining popularity at weddings. It's a shade that pairs beautifully with almost every color imaginable and works in any setting and season. As the softer version of black, it acts as a neutral, but when paired with the ultimate neutral—white—it really stands out on its own. Gray works especially well in urban settings and loftlike venues and makes materials like concrete or steel look downright refined. Its versatile range from soft cloudy gray to deep charcoal means it works for any level of formality. Like white, gray's undertones change with the slightest hint of another color. Gray can skew purple, blue, red, brown, and even green, so it's critical to keep swatches with you and to order samples of anything before placing the final order.

FLOWERS Corsages

While not necessary, corsages are a lovely way to recognize the immediate family of the couple, including parents, stepparents, grandparents, and any siblings not in the bridal party. They can even be extended to people taking part in the wedding, such as ceremony readers. They're also a nice alternative to the bridesmaids' bouquets, especially if you're working with a tight floral budget. Some weddings we've seen have offered small flower corsages to their female guests, which is a nice touch.

Remember, corsages don't have to be made of real flowers. When done in fabric or even paper, they can become wonderful keepsakes.

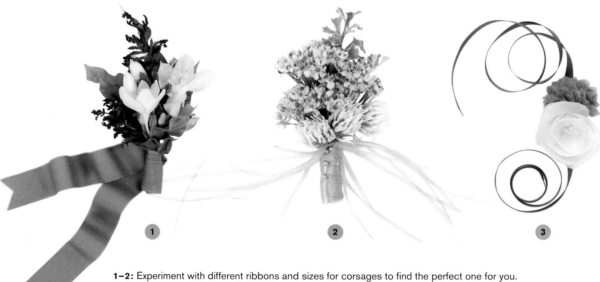

1–2: Experiment with different ribbons and sizes for corsages to find the perfect one for you.
3: For corsages that last, fabric or paper versions can double as keepsakes for their wearers.

OPPOSITE: Corsages are a nice way to recognize the lovely ladies in your life.
For a modern take, they can even replace the bridesmaids' bouquets!

Bridal accessories

FASHION

Brides today have so many options for accessorizing, it can be hard to choose! The great thing is that a simple white dress with little adornment is the perfect canvas for adding some color and personality.

Accessorizing can also be practical. For example, if your church venue requests that shoulders remain covered, a shrug or jacket is a must for a strapless dress. If you're planning a winter wedding, you might want a jacket or faux-fur stole instead of a winter coat. A purse or clutch is a necessity for the essentials like lipstick, breath mints, and of course a cell phone for some wedding day selfies! Even if you don't carry it the whole night, it is good to have a place for all your necessities, and it's a nice excuse to buy a new purse. A sash is the perfect add-on to a simple dress. A colored satin ribbon from the craft store is the most budget friendly, but you can go all the way up to handmade ribbon flowers or beaded sashes for a little more pizzazz. Your sash can be worn for the whole day or added on at the reception if you feel like giving your dress a mini makeover. An often-overlooked accessory is the glove, but gloves can be a stunning add-on. Remember Carolyn Bessette-Kennedy's sheer just-below-the-elbow-length gloves paired with her simple Narciso Rodriguez gown? It was stunning and so modern! That length was perfect since her arms were fully exposed and her dress was full length, but a short pair would work equally as well with a cocktail-length dress or a dress with short sleeves.

1: A floral sash can be added after the ceremony to give your dress a new look for the reception. 2: This ostrich clutch is the perfect way to keep all of your day-of essentials close. 3: An embroidered clutch makes the ultimate gift for your bridesmaids. 4: For a winter wedding, this stylish jacket can be worn to and from the venue without messing up your dress.

OPPOSITE: Sometimes just the simplest bit of color can drastically change the look of a wedding dress. This shimmery gray cover-up and ostrich-feathered clutch are beyond chic and can be worn after the wedding as well!

PAPER Menus

Menus aren't a die-hard necessity, but they sure add a nice touch to your reception. While you may have already requested your guests' meal preference in the invitation, the menu elaborates on the offerings. If done right, it can also be a memorable design element or special keepsake that your guests will want to take home. Typically, menus are a single-sided card printed with the meal options as well as wine pairings and drink options. If you decide to print a menu for each place setting, order these at least six weeks ahead of your wedding date. Allow a little extra time if you choose to do any die cutting, such as having the menu cut in the shape of the plate, since this process takes a bit longer.

Another unique idea is having the menu printed on the napkins at each setting. Companies like Spoonflower will print any design onto a variety of fabrics, or else you can take matters into your own hands and screen print fabrics yourself. An oversized menu displayed in plain sight has a big impact and can be more cost effective than individual menus. You can also opt to display a couple of small menus at the bar to highlight signature cocktails. And don't forget the kids! If children are invited to the reception, merging the menu into an interactive coloring book will keep them occupied and allow parents to enjoy their meal with limited interruption.

OPPOSITE: Customizing your napkins with the menu at your reception is easier than you think, and your guests will be delighted by the thoughtful detail!

Gemma & Lawrence

DINNER MENU
BROOKLYN, NEW YORK

Starters

RADISH AND CUCUMBER CROSTINI
WITH DILL BUTTER & SEA SALT

TRI-COLOR BEET SALAD
WITH BLUE CHEESE

Mains

SEASONAL FISH WITH
FRESH HERBS & LEMONS

CORNISH HEN SEASONED WITH
ROSEMARY & THYME

GRILLED VEGETABLES

Sides

FINGERLING POTATOES

GRILLED ASPARAGUS

Sweets

WEDDING CAKE

ASSORTED MINI COOKIES,
BROWNIES & TARTLETS

Cocktail

BLACKBERRY BRAMBLE WITH
FRESHLY MUDDLED BLACKBERRIES,
CITRUS & CRUSHED ICE

An oversized menu is perfect
for large, open spaces and
doubles as a décor element.

Let your guests know about your signature cocktails with a sleek menu displayed at the bar.

Make your menu multifunctional by having it double as a vessel for centerpieces.

A beautiful watercolor menu makes the perfect accompaniment to a tasteful place setting.

Keep your younger guests occupied with a menu that doubles as a coloring book. Make sure to have plenty of crayons and pencils available!

Wedding cakes

One of the final shots of your wedding day will likely be you getting wedding cake smashed in your face by your spouse, so the cake is an element with high photographic potential. So much can be accomplished with cakes these days: realistic sugar flowers, jewels, gilding, sky-high tiers . . . if you can dream it up, chances are your baker can make it happen.

Ideally your cake will match the formality and décor of the wedding, but inspiration can come from anywhere. Check out magazines or Pinterest to start formulating some ideas but also look to other elements such as your dress or bouquet. Details such as lace or beading can be replicated in edible form, or you can use pretty edible flowers as decoration if you don't want sugar florals.

Look into bakers as soon as you settle on a venue and style for the wedding. Prepare to stuff your face at your cake tasting! This is arguably the best part of selecting the wedding cake, since you get to try all different flavors and fillings.

The two most popular coverings for cake are buttercream and fondant. Buttercream can be applied in many ways, from perfect to perfectly imperfect, and can be easily redone if there's any damage. Fondant, on the other hand, is a rolled sugar paste very similar to dough that gets draped over the cake. It's great for really creative decorative cakes because it can be dyed to any color and shaped in a multitude of ways, but most people don't find it very tasty. The nice thing about fondant is that it needs to be applied with a layer of butter-cream underneath, so guests can just peel it off if they don't want to eat it. A new trend is the naked cake, which has no exterior icing at all. The result is definitely a more rustic look, but it's a nice (and tasty) new take on the traditional wedding cake.

While historically wedding cakes are made of white cake and icing, they can really be any flavor you choose. From chocolate to carrot cake, whipped cream topping to custard filling, try out different pairings to find your favorite. If you want a traditional cake but want to serve another flavor as well, you can also do a groom's cake, which is generally made with chocolate or fruit (but can be any flavor). Groom's cakes are usually a more whimsical cake, reflecting the groom's interests, such as a sports team, favorite pet, or hobby, and are served from a separate table than that of the main wedding cake.

Many couples save the top tier of their cake so they can enjoy it on their one-year anniversary. Ask your caterer to prep it for you and then put it straight into your freezer for storing. Some cakes may not make it for the full year without drying out or just not tasting as fresh as on your wedding day, so a lot of couples will forgo saving the original tier and just order a new one from the baker to enjoy on their first anniversary.

NEXT SPREAD: Your cake can take on nearly any design—from materials like marble or chalkboard, to ombré ruffles, glittery stripes, scallops, and simple polka dots. For inspiration, take a closer look at your venue, dress, invitation, city, and flowers to see if there's something there that can direct the design.

LOVE is sweet

CHALKBOARD AND water PAPER FLOWERS

SCALLOPED border

Grey MARBLE

riley + gregory

2016

Rolling
DOTS

Glitter
STRIPES

OMBRE
layers

Photo display STYLING

Often at ceremonies or receptions, couples want to show off some of their lovely engagement photos, share their parents' or grandparents' wedding photos, or display photos to honor important family or friends who couldn't be in attendance. A styled display is a special way to share cherished memories and people with your guests.

When using photos from different eras, start off by having them all reprinted in black-and-white so they'll match in tone. Washi tape is your best friend when it comes to creating makeshift frames that won't damage your venue's walls. Grab a bunch of different patterns and widths and go to town framing your photos. If your space has some height, order helium-filled balloons to hold your photos just above eye level, or right at eye level if they'll be displayed where guests won't get tangled up in them. It's easy to dress up simple white frames with gift wrap or artist's paper (plus, you can reuse the frames in your home or gift them to relatives). If your venue won't let you hang anything on the walls, use some tabletop easels or just lean frames against the wall. Photos are the best way to personalize your wedding.

1: High ceilings can handle larger-scale displays. A fun option is filling up an area with balloons and attaching photos to their strings. **2:** Give inexpensive frames a snazzy update with gift wrap. Just cut a piece to size and use it as a mat for the photos. **3:** Displaying meaningful objects along with photos in a little cloche looks sweet and will keep your guests looking.

OPPOSITE: For an easy photo display that won't damage your venue's walls, print your engagement photos large and affix them to the walls with decorative washi tape.

please
SIGN OUR
GUEST BOOK!

BE MY GUEST

Clay tags

If you're looking for a personalized way to wrap little favors or a sweet way to decorate your bouquet, try making customized clay tags. They're easy to make with oven-bake clay, and they make darling keepsakes.

WHAT YOU'LL NEED

- 2 sheets of parchment paper (enough to cover your work surface and baking sheet)
- 1 roll of artist's tape
- 2 oz/55 g oven-bake clay in black and 2 oz/55 g in white (We used Premo! Sculpey.)
- Rolling pin (Acrylic works best but a wooden pin works, too.)
- Cookie cutters in various shapes
- Thin flat spatula
- 1 wooden skewer
- Various stamps of letters and numbers
- Baking sheet
- Twine or ribbon

1. Secure a large piece of parchment paper to your work surface, securing the edges with artist's tape. Tear off another piece to cover your baking sheet; set aside for later.

2. Preheat the oven to 275°F/135°C.

3. Start with the white clay. Unwrap the entire piece and knead with your hands to soften it up. Roll the clay into a cigar shape and set aside.

4. Take one section of the black clay and knead to soften it. (This particular brand divides the clay into four sections.) Roll the piece into a smaller cigar shape and then combine with your white clay.

5. Twist and knead the two colors together, occasionally rolling out the clay with the rolling pin to see how the marbled design is coming together. When you're happy with the marbled design, roll the clay out with the rolling pin until it is about ⅛ in/3 mm thick. Using your cookie cutters, start cutting out shapes in areas where the marbling is best.

6. With the flat spatula, transfer the shapes to the parchment-covered cookie sheet.

7. Collect the remaining clay scraps into a ball, roll out again with the rolling pin, and repeat cutting out shapes until you've used up all the clay.

8. Take your letter and number stamps and with a steady hand, stamp into the clay. Your tags could say a simple "Thanks" or something more personal such as your wedding date or initials.

9. With the thicker end of the wooden skewer, poke a hole through the clay at the top of the tag.

10. Pop the cookie sheet with your tags into the oven and bake for 30 minutes or according to the clay package instructions.

11. When the tags are done, allow them to cool and then attach to your items with twine or ribbon.

TIP
- Test out your stamping skills on a scrap piece of clay so you can get used to the pressure needed for a clean impression.

Ask the expert

BETSY THORLEIFSON OF NINE CAKES

Betsy Thorleifson started Nine Cakes in the fall of 2008 after years of baking for friends and family. Fueled by her passion for food, handcrafted goods, and collaborating with others, Betsy continues to build a reputation for beautiful and delicious cakes through Nine Cakes.

Q: When should a couple meet with their baker? What information should they have with them for the meeting?
A: Couples should meet with their baker four to six months ahead of the wedding. They should already have their venue booked, know approximately how many guests will attend, and be able to share the overall vision and inspiration for their wedding.

Q: How should couples settle on a flavor? What are some great unexpected flavor pairings?
A: Couples should first and foremost choose a flavor they love and not worry too much about pleasing everyone or choosing something "safe." Choosing flavor pairings that are unique, based on seasonal flavors, or that complement the dinner menu are great approaches.

Some unique pairings I love: Ginger cake with lime curd and fresh ginger buttercream; almond cardamom cake with fresh pear purée and Poire William buttercream; vanilla cake with layers of salted caramel, peanut butter buttercream, and chocolate ganache; dark chocolate cake with Mexican chocolate buttercream and cacao nibs; pistachio cake with orange zested cream cheese and fresh strawberries . . . I could go on forever!

Q: How do you figure out the size of the cake based on portions? What's an average size for a cake for a wedding reception of 150?
A: Each tier has a different number of servings. There are many ways to configure a cake to serve 150. I've done four tiers for a slightly wider cake and six tiers for a narrower but taller cake. One of my favorite options is to do multiple tiers in different heights—so maybe it's a six-tiered cake, but some of the tiers are half or twice as tall as a standard-sized tier.

Q: What are the pros and cons of buttercream versus fondant?
A: Buttercream lends a more natural look to the cake. I like to leave some texture to buttercream, but you can also achieve a very smooth finish. Fondant gives a sleeker, modern feel with a flawless finish. I love using it for cakes with a modern design and kids' cakes.

Q: What's the best way to save the top of your cake for your first anniversary?
A: Once the cake is chilled, wrap it airtight in layers of plastic wrap and a final layer of aluminum foil, and then place in the freezer. On your anniversary, remove the cake well in advance of when you'd like to serve the cake, so that it's nice and soft at room temperature.

Q: Be honest: how do you feel about cupcakes?
A: A cupcake is perfect for when you're out and about and need a sweet treat. But special occasions call for special cakes! In the same way it's meaningful to share a meal with your family and friends, I feel the same way about sharing a cake. Whether a child's birthday or a wedding, there's just something more intimate about everyone having a slice of cake. A slice of decadent cake served to your guests is a lovely ritual and creates a shared experience, and for me cupcakes just don't hold the same significance.

Q: What do you love about your job?
A: I love that the work stays fresh because there are always new cakes to work on: each couple presents new ideas, new challenges to figure out, and new prettiness to achieve. I also love coming up with new flavor pairings. Eating amazing food and desserts is a sensual experience, and that definitely makes for a good wedding cake. I love the look on someone's face when they eat our cake. It's rewarding to be part of someone's wedding day and part of making their experience delightful.

Q: Quick fire: Cupcakes or cake?
A: Cake.

Q: Quick fire: Fondant or buttercream?
A: Buttercream.

Q: Quick fire: Topper or no topper?
A: No topper. I just prefer whatever the design of the cake is to carry up to the top, unless the topper somehow ties in with the design.

Q: Quick fire: First slice—feed to your partner gracefully or smash it in his or her face?
A: Gracefully.

Q: If you were a color, what color would you be?
A: Blueberry.

MRS. and MRS.

Metallic

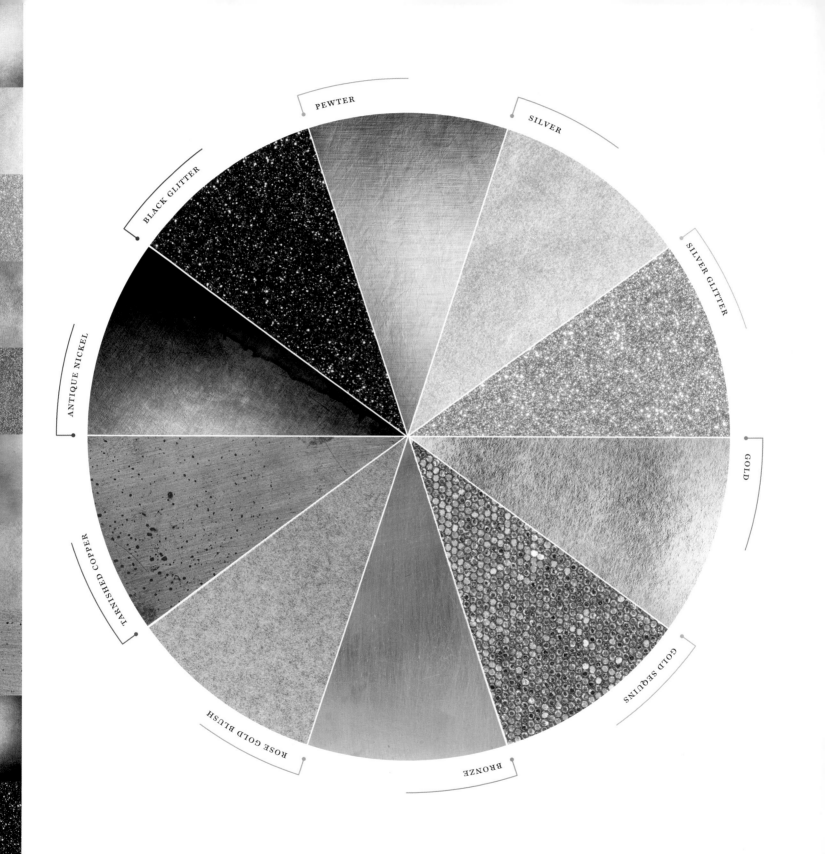

Palette

Nothing says glitz and glamour quite like a metallic! No wonder metallics are so popular for evening events. Almost every color has a metallic counterpart, but for this chapter, we focus on the standards: gold, silver, copper, and bronze. Within each of these colors are various shades and finishes, from brushed to satin to polished. Mixing the four gives you a rich palette of tones. In the past, it was a bit taboo to mix metals, but those days are over. When done right, combining metals looks stunning.

Gold, depending on how it's done, can have a modern or old-world effect, which makes it incredibly versatile. It's a color that exudes wealth and luxury and begs to be looked at. It also says "party." While gold works well in formal weddings and during the evening hours, there's no reason it can't work for any wedding setting. Silver is far more soothing and relaxed. It's not as flashy as gold and, therefore, becomes a great neutral when paired with other brighter colors. When done with just white, silver is cool and sleek—a combination that works especially well in the winter months. Copper and bronze have quietly worked their way into the design world over the last few years. A wedding featuring either of these metallics will be on trend and modern. Copper and bronze also skew toward an industrial look, which is great for loftlike venues.

FLOWERS
Creative centerpieces

As we briefly touched upon in the Green chapter, centerpieces don't have to be floral to be impactful. Sometimes, in fact, alternative centerpieces are more impactful by the sheer fact that they are unexpected! Besides, it's rare to find naturally gold flowers in nature, so get ready to break out the spray paint.

When creating centerpieces in your desired palette, you can spray just about anything from fake flowers to leaves, fruit, toys, vintage finds, even simple wooden shapes. Spraying items unifies them and creates an incredibly modern look. To differentiate some objects, add glitter so that they'll glimmer and pop when the light hits just right, or play around alternating matte and glossy paint finishes. If spray painting isn't your thing, you could take something as humble as a cardboard cube and decorate it in different ways: wrap it in metallic gift wrap or take a bunch of glittery ribbons and wrap them around the cube. A series of these stacked in the center of the reception table in varying sizes can really add some interest.

Candleholders and candelabras can make a big statement for centerpieces. You could choose something as simple as a votive wrapped in strips of Mylar tape to a table full of faceted taper holders with the slightest hint of metallic. Instead of thinking of centerpieces just on the table, consider how to work in décor from the ceiling. Just imagine how a ceiling full of glimmering paper stars would look filling up your reception venue!

1: A collection of faceted candlesticks with simple white tapers are the ultimate in modern décor.
2: Spray-painted and glittered fruit in a matching vessel makes for a stunning still-life centerpiece.
3: Paper lanterns don't need to hang to be a great centerpiece. Arrange a few in the center of the table in different sizes for a festive look.

OPPOSITE: Consider centerpieces from above as well as below. These stars are a great way to fill the space when paired with simple white candle centerpieces on the table. We went with a monochromatic look here in all gold, but it works because of the mix of textures: the sleek shininess of the stars and fortune cookies with the fringy drink stirrers and matte sequins of the tablecloth.

Jewelry

When it comes to wedding fashion, accessorizing with jewelry presents lots of options. Of course, none is as important as the engagement ring! Some brides spend years dreaming of that moment when they get presented with the perfect ring, while others wait to be pleasantly surprised. And while many of you probably have a rock on your finger already, here are some tips to share with the men in your life as they start the search for the perfect ring.

With so many rings out there, it can be a daunting task to find "the one." Pay attention to stone shapes like cushion, solitaire, emerald, princess, and pear, and note the different metals used for the rings. Gold is a classic, but platinum has risen in the ranks since it is hypoallergenic and incredibly durable. Next, think about the stone and start getting schooled in the 4Cs (*cut*, *color*, *clarity*, and *carat*). Often settings and stones are sold separately, so be sure to ask the jeweler lots of questions. There's no reason why the engagement ring has to be a diamond. Many brides today rock emeralds, sapphires, rubies, and even opals. Throw tradition out the window and wear something you love! Figuring out a budget is the next step. It used to be the standard rule to spend two months' salary on the ring, but this is no longer the case. Just spend what you can without going into debt. You can get creative by getting slightly less than the full carat without it being noticeable, or surrounding a stone in the center with smaller ones so it looks larger.

Once the engagement ring is on and you're ready to tie the knot, it's time to look for wedding bands. This is something you should do together. Settle on a budget (a good number to start with is about 3 percent of your wedding budget) and then hit the stores. Plain bands are significantly less in cost than ones that incorporate stones or multiple metals.

OPPOSITE: Jewelry is a great gift for your bridesmaids and flower girls. Select matching pieces or find individual pieces that suit each of their personalities.

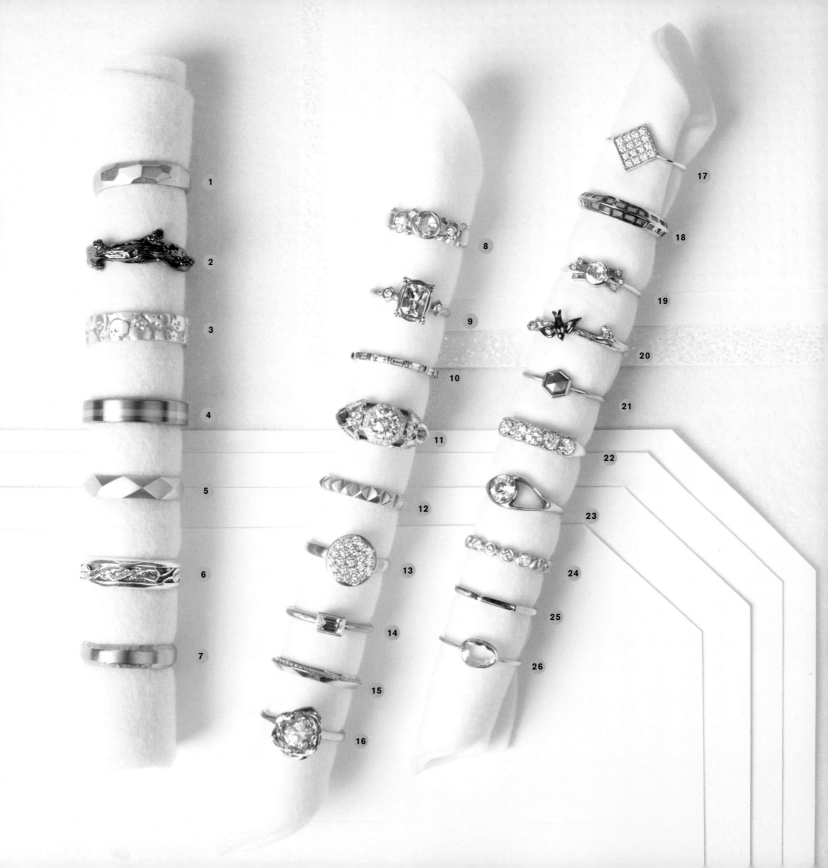

Also, no rule that says your rings have to match, but think long term about your lifestyle. A straight-edged ring might look really modern now, but could be uncomfortable, so it may not be the best choice for something you'll wear for a lifetime. Try not to leave the shopping until the last minute since some rings can take up to a month to be ready, especially if they're custom-made or have any engraving on the inside.

After you have your dress and veil picked out, it's time to shop for some fun jewels to accessorize with! If your dress is overly elaborate (especially at the top) you might want to forget about a necklace and go with some great chandelier earrings instead. But if your dress is simple and sleek, a big statement necklace may be just what you need to complete the look. Try to stick with similar metals and styles. A bright white dress looks great with silvers and platinums, while more ivory shades go better with yellow gold. Another idea is to borrow a family heirloom as your "something old." If all the options get to be too much, you can't go wrong with simple diamond studs or pearls.

OPPOSITE: You are going to wear your engagement ring and wedding band every day, so make sure they fit your personality and style. Experiment with different stones, shapes, metals, and throw out the idea that your ring has to conform to any one look.

1: Carla Caruso, 14k white gold; **2:** Jennifer Yi, 14k black gold; **3:** Donovan Smith, 14k white gold; **4:** Jerry Spaulding, titanium, 18k yellow gold; **5:** Carla Caruso, 14k yellow gold; **6:** Jennifer Yi, 14k white gold; **7:** Rebecca Overmann, 14k white gold; **8:** Donovan Smith, 14k yellow gold, diamonds; **9:** Megan Thorne, 18k white gold, white sapphire, diamonds; **10:** Bario Neal, 14k rose gold, diamonds, **11:** Jennifer Yi, platinum, diamond, sapphires; **12:** Carla Caruso, 14k yellow gold; **13:** Caroline Ellen, 20k yellow gold, diamonds, **14:** Annie Fensterstock, platinum, 22k yellow gold, diamond; **15:** Nicholas Liu, 18k yellow gold, diamonds; **16:** Jennifer Yi, 14k rose gold, zircon; **17:** Erica Weiner, 14k yellow and white gold, diamonds; **18:** Nicholas Liu, 18k yellow gold; **19:** Erica Weiner, 14k yellow and white gold, diamonds; **20:** Jennifer Yi, 18k rose and black gold; **21:** Rebecca Overmann, 14k yellow gold, diamond; **22:** Erica Weiner, 14k yellow and white gold, diamonds; **23:** Bario Neal, platinum, diamond; **24:** Marian Maurer, 18k yellow gold, diamonds; **25:** Bario Neal, 18k yellow gold; **26:** Sarah McGuire, 18k yellow gold, white sapphire.

NEXT SPREAD: Your jewelry options are limitless and should only be dictated by what you feel best in. Paired with the right dress, any of these options would be stunners.

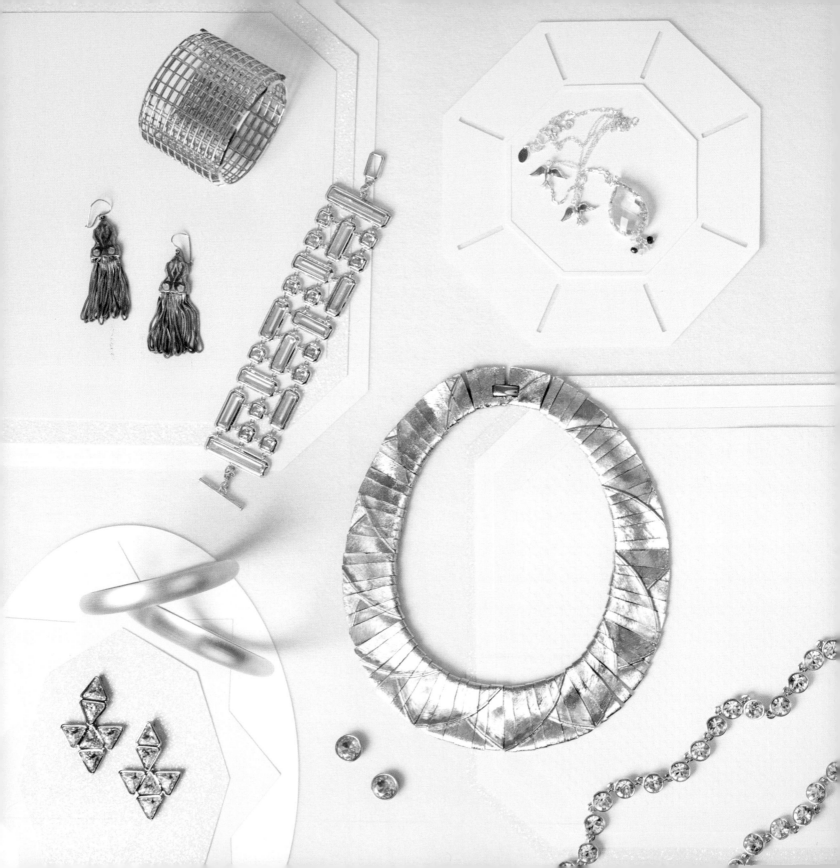

Seating charts & escort cards

No matter the size of your reception, if you're having a sit-down dinner, you'll need a seating chart or escort cards. Otherwise, your guests won't know where to sit, and all those agonizing hours of arranging and rearranging your seating chart will go to waste! You have many options, from just having a seating chart, to doing a seating chart with place cards, to just using escort cards. Couples are getting more and more creative when it comes to this particular bit of signage, and with good reason—often guests want to take the cards home with them at the end of the night.

What's the difference between an escort card and a place card? An escort card is usually found at the entrance to the reception during cocktail hour and will have a guest's name and table number on it. Once the guest finds the table, he can sit anywhere. A place card, on the other hand, tells each guest exactly which seat is hers, and it is usually placed directly at her place setting. The place card works particularly well in conjunction with a seating chart so that guests can at least know which table to look for when finding their names. A seating chart without escort or place cards works better for smaller receptions.

The seating chart and escort/place cards can be as simple or elaborate as you want them to be. Some brides don't want to dedicate a lot of time to this and are perfectly content to have the names simply printed or written with calligraphy on the cards and arranged neatly. But others see this as a unique moment for your guests as they enter the reception. Any opportunity to make an element of your wedding a keepsake is a good one!

OPPOSITE: Chrome gift bows clustered in a multitude of sizes make for a striking seating announcement. Add the smallest bow to each of your escort cards.

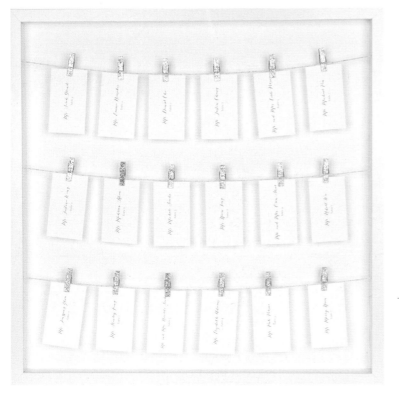

Your guests are all winners with these mini trophy escort cards. Trophies can be found at your local party store or online. We printed the escort cards and draped them through the trophies' arms.

A simple white frame finds new life as an escort card display with the help of some metallic twine and hand-glittered mini clothespins. An easy DIY for maximum effect!

We took a standard printed seating chart and added scallops made from metallic contact paper to give it an art deco look. The glitter letters were created using a Cricut machine, but these can easily be duplicated with a craft knife and a steady hand.

Your escort cards can take so many shapes and patterns. Choosing a fun mix has an eclectic playful feel. (Also see facing.)

Hors d'oeuvres presentation

If you ask wedding guests what they remember most about a wedding, they'll usually tell you two things: the music and the food. So it's not only important that the food tastes good, but it should look good, too. Metallics are a little difficult to incorporate into food since they're generally not found as natural edibles. However, you can work around this with some creativity.

One simple way is to display food on metallic chargers. The plates are large enough to hold enough passed hors d'oeuvres for several people, and the metallic elevates the look. Clear Lucite trays can get an upgrade with a simple DIY: spray the underside of the tray generously with spray adhesive, then sprinkle glitter and let dry. A less-messy version is to use a glittery paper or even gift wrap on the underside. And don't forget the humble cocktail napkin or food pick. Napkins can be foiled with initials, dates, or phrases, and picks come in a variety of fun colors and shapes to work for any appetizer.

To add a bit more glitz, consider using glittery rock salt, sprinkles, sugars, or dragée's as beds for food as well (just make sure that the container holding them has a high enough edge so they don't spill everywhere). Or try decorating the food itself with bits of edible gold or silver. Glasses or small bowls can be rimmed with edible glitter. Your caterer will be able to help brainstorm even more ideas for working metallics into the menu.

When working on the game plan for your cocktail hour with the caterer, provide a variety of food options for your guests. Have a mix of vegetarian and nonvegetarian options, throw in some cheese and charcuterie, and offer bites that vary in temperature and texture to keep it interesting. The cocktail hour is a great time to work in your favorite comfort foods in miniature, like tiny sliders, mini tacos, or mac-and-cheese bites. These are guaranteed crowd-pleasers! The majority of the hors d'oeuvres should be passed, and limit any food stations, as they just end up with long lines. If you do use food stations, have items that don't require plates that guests have to carry around with them afterward.

OPPOSITE: Metallic chargers, picks, napkins, and even trays lined with gift wrap can all add some shine to your appetizers. And don't forget the edible gold or silver leaf . . . a little goes a long way!

ABOVE: Coasters with foiled designs make an eye-catching display item.

STYLING

Celebration

Honestly, your wedding may be the biggest celebration of your life. And to celebrate is to include your loved ones. You can find lots of fun ways to do this. If you have a lot of children you want to include in the wedding party, have them walk down the aisle ahead of you with signs announcing your arrival. This is always a great photo op!

Traditionally as the couple exits after saying "I Do," guests have done all sorts of things, from ringing bells to throwing rice or birdseed. But why not take a cue from birthday parties and New Year's Eve and up the fun by passing out some party horns? (Just be careful any kids at the wedding don't get their hands on them during the ceremony!) Or pass out mini bottles of bubbles wrapped with ribbon in your color scheme for guests to blow as you walk away. It's simple DIY and less mess than throwing rice. Plus, it looks dreamy, and kids love it.

As far as celebrating at the reception, one fun idea is to set up a confetti bar during cocktail hour. We came up with this idea a few years ago for an event, and it was a huge hit! All you need are some containers, bulk confetti, glassine bags, and some scoops or spoons. Set it up where guests can come and fill the bags with a bit of confetti. Then either have them toss it at your send-off or keep it as a favor. It's a nice way to take the celebration home! If you're looking for a ready-made option, you can find confetti poppers on the Internet that you can easily customize in your palette. Just make sure that your venue doesn't have a clause against using confetti; it can be a pain to clean up, so some places don't allow it.

OPPOSITE: If you have small children to include in the ceremony but already have a ring bearer and flower girl, ask a few of the other children to march down the aisle with cute signs to let guests know that you're on your way.

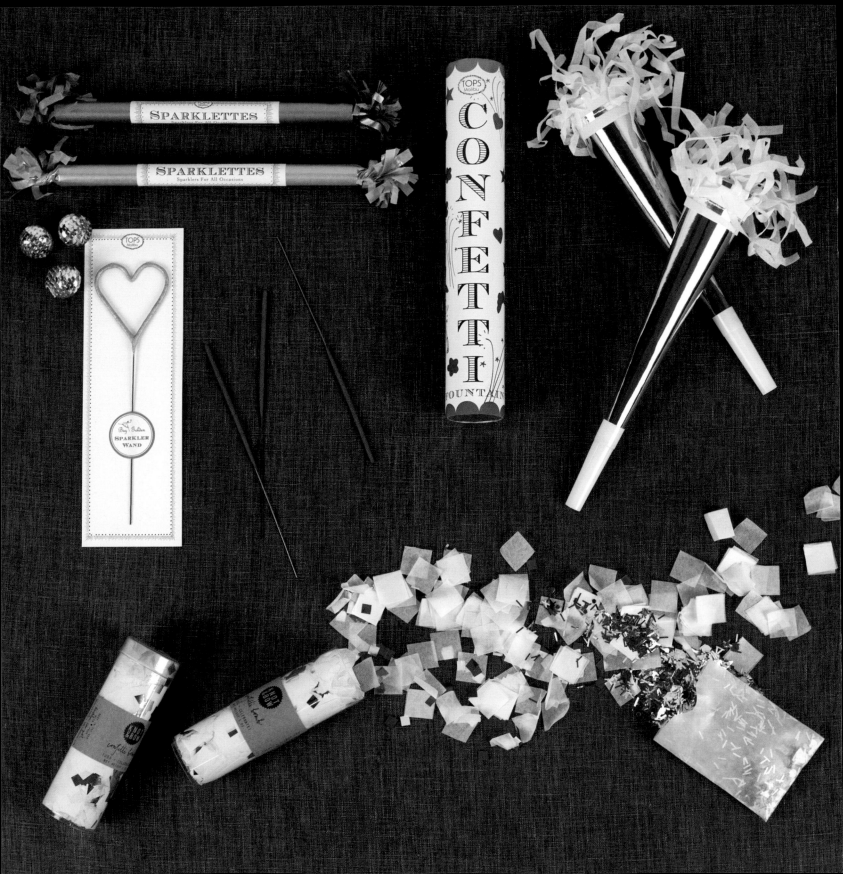

Sparklers are a perfect send-off for evening weddings. Keep baskets near the exit with the sparklers and souvenir matches for your guests to grab. Once your send-off is done, make sure to have containers of sand on hand to extinguish them. Again, you'll want to check with your venue to make sure sparklers are allowed; if they are, definitely consider using them because they make for great photos!

OPPOSITE: Sparklers, horns, and confetti are just some of the ways to celebrate in a big way.
ABOVE LEFT: A confetti bar is a fun activity and makes for an equally sweet send-off.
ABOVE RIGHT: Mini balloon letters are super-festive, especially when used in photos.

Mylar-wrapped frames

This DIY is incredibly easy, and it can be used in many ways for your wedding, from table numbers to signage to photo display. The frames also make great favors or keepsakes.

WHAT YOU'LL NEED

- Table number printouts (www.chroniclebooks .com/weddingsincolor), photos, or other items for display
- Printer (optional)
- 12-by-12-in/30.5-by-30.5-cm sheets of glitter paper in the color of your choice (The number of sheets needed depends on the size of your numbers and how many you need to make.)

- Scissors
- Magnetic acrylic frames of various sizes (available at Crate & Barrel and other home stores)
- Rolls of gold and silver Mylar tape in varying widths (We used widths of ¾ in/2 cm and ¼ in/6 mm.)

1. Draw or print out the numbers at a size that works with your frames. Place your numbers over the glitter paper and, using the scissors, cut them out as neatly as possible.

2. Open your acrylic frame and situate the number in it. Make sure the number is as close to centered as possible. Then without disturbing the number, align the magnets to close the frame.

3. Take your larger gold tape and, starting at one end of the frame, apply it as close to the edge as possible. The tape is easy to lift up and doesn't leave a residue, so if you need to start over, that's okay. Once you've affixed the tape all the way around the frame, use the scissors to cut a clean edge. Depending on the width of your frame, you may need to go around twice with the tape.

4. Once you have a base of tape around all of the edges of the frame, you can either leave the frame as is or add another thin layer to hide the seam. You can also add decorative strips of another color all the way around. There's no wrong way to do this!

Ask the expert CATERING

JEREMY WACHALTER OF COBBLESTONE CATERING

After graduating from the Culinary Institute of America and before launching Cobblestone Catering, Jeremy Wachalter worked as a sous-chef at The Modern in New York City. He also worked at Town, Union Pacific, and had a short stint at Napa Valley's Tra Vigne. His self-described style is "French and Italian, with some Asian-inspired touches" and his retail shop, headquartered in Cobble Hill, Brooklyn, reflects the instincts of a chef who places the utmost importance on quality and seasonality. Cobblestone Catering recently opened a tasting room in Manhattan, dedicated to entertaining private clients. Jeremy had the honor of becoming a Fellow at the Culinary Institute of America in 2014.

Q: What are some go-to crowd-pleasers for wedding menus?
A: Mini classics with an upgrade. For example, Truffled Grilled Cheese, Lobster Mac + Cheese, BBQ Brisket Sliders, Spicy Duck Meatballs, Mini Cones of French Fries, or Waffle Potato Chips.

Q: What's the best way to inject the couple's personality when it comes to food?
A: A family recipe or dishes based on the couple's travels are great ways to incorporate a very personal touch. We always ask our clients their favorite restaurants and dishes. Often, I will go eat at the restaurants and have the actual dishes my clients rave about so I can re-create them for the wedding.

Q: Are tables, place settings, glassware, and linens provided by caterers or is that a separate service? What if the bride and groom want to bring their own?
A: Most of the time these are provided by an outside rental company. We do not offer this service at all. Some events require two or even three different rental companies for the various elements. Some companies have great chandeliers and some have great linens—it's best to work with a few to get the best results. We love when couples incorporate their own special touches to the décor.

Q: How far in advance should couples establish the menu final counts? How to deal with last-minute requests?
A: At Cobblestone, menus can be changed up to fourteen days before an event. Final count is seven days before the event. We see it as our business to accommodate bridal parties and their guests, and we really try to accommodate any adjustments that we can.

Q: What's the average cost per person for a sit-down meal? What are some cost-cutting tricks?

A: The average cost really depends on the food but can range from $75 to $175 per person. The number of courses and individual menu choices play a big role in the overall budget. Some great ways to keep within budget are to go with fewer courses and keep everything simple and plated. People tend to think a buffet will be cheaper, but the catering company ends up having to produce more food, so it's actually not cost effective.

Q: How soon should you start meeting with potential caterers, and when should you do your tasting? What do you do if your caterer doesn't do tastings?

A: Good catering companies are generally booked a full year out. Therefore, the caterer should be one of the very first vendors hired. Try to get in for a tasting as soon as possible. Quite honestly, I would never work with a company who doesn't do tastings. This doesn't feel very accommodating and doesn't seem consistent with the type of relationship you want with a very important vendor.

Q: Quick fire: Open bar or signature cocktail?

A: Both. I am in the food business, and I love to drink and eat, so I would have both of these. For those who don't care much for drinking, it's fine to pick one or the other. Take into consideration that not everyone will like the "signature drink," so you may want to have two or three, maybe one that the groom creates and one that the bride creates.

Q: Quick fire: Sit-down dinner or buffet?

A: Sit-down; no comparison. When I think of buffets, I think of my bar mitzvah. You compromise the quality of the food in the buffet. I would avoid buffets altogether and maybe opt for family style if plated is too formal.

Q: Quick fire: Savory or sweet?

A: Savory. Nourish your guests and offer a few sweets at the end.

Q: If you were a color, what color would you be?

A: Black. All other colors look great against black.

Acknowledgments

We are so happy to be able to share this book with you, and it would not have been possible without our fabulous team! Thank you to our editor, Laura Lee Mattingly, who saw the potential in pushing the modern aesthetic for weddings and got this book off the ground, and to our agent, Melissa Flashman.

Thank you to our beautiful models: Lindsay Brunk, Lindsey Madden, Elizabeth Rees, Jenna Hein, Falcon Griffith, and Anne Brown. And to the debut models, little Truman Cho Jr. and his friend London Darrell. To Amanda and Najeebah from Face Time Beauty for their amazing hair and makeup talents. To all the designers, calligraphers, and stationers who created pieces especially for the book, we thank you! To our roster of star wedding experts who lent their time, talents, and expertise, we are forever grateful: Betsy Thorleifson, Sarah Brysk Cohen, Xochitl Gonzalez, Linsey and Jeremy Wachalter, Gabriella Risatti, and Daniel and Brenna Lewis. To our intern, Teny Eurdekian. To our stylist, Michelle Edgemont, who styled this book beautifully under extreme duress (read: pregnant!), and her assistant Michelle Bablo. To our amazing photographer, Jainé Kershner of Brklyn View Photography, for bringing this book to life with her assistants Eileen Meny and Newt Kershner. And of course, to our husbands, Chad and Truman, who acted as our personal errand boys for months on end with very little complaint!

VB: Additionally, I'd like to thank everyone at GVID who put up with my insanity all these months. To my dear friends whom I've neglected horribly (virtual and not), but were always in my corner cheering me on, I'll be forever grateful and owe you all a drink. To my parents (who are probably ecstatic I'm finally putting my English degree to good use!), thank you for all the years of love and support you've given me. And to my husband, Chad, thanks for letting me turn the apartment into a storage unit filled with boxes of wedding cakes, confetti, balloons, dresses, and other wedding paraphernalia. Though in all honesty, if you hadn't proposed all those years ago, there would be no *Brooklyn Bride*, thus no book, so you have no one to blame but yourself.

MC: I would like to thank my parents for supporting me when I told them I wanted to be an artist and not pushing me to be a doctor or lawyer like many Korean parents often do! An especially big thank you to my dad for the advice of giving graphic design a chance even when I had my heart set on being a painter. I wouldn't have found the path that led me here today if it wasn't for your words of encouragement. Also a big shout out to my husband, Truman, my biggest cheerleader—thank you so much for all the times you built our tradeshow booths, the countless nights spent folding and packing orders, and for not getting "mad" when I constantly lose my keys. Without your push, we would have never started this company, and I am forever grateful. And to my little Tru, you are my joy and reason for working so hard. Lastly to God, for this beautiful life and world that is ever so amazing and full of inspiration.

Credits

Red/Pink

FLOWERS: THE BOUQUET
Flowers:
Blossom and Branch
www.blossomandbranch.com

Ribbon:
M&J Trimming
www.mjtrim.com

FASHION: WEDDING DAY MAKEUP
Nail polish:
Essie
www.essie.com

Camisole:
Journelle
www.journelle.com

Hair accessories:
Ban.do
www.shopbando.com

Corset top:
Ann Taylor
www.anntaylor.com

Earrings:
Kate Spade
www.katespade.com

Makeup and hair: Face Time Beauty
www.facetimebeauty.com

PAPER: UNIQUE INVITATIONS
Laser-cut acrylic invitations:
The Crafty Smiths
www.etsy.com/shop /TheCraftySmiths

Watercolor invite with paper cut dolls:
Julie Song Ink
www.juliesongink.com

Handkerchief invite:
custom design, printed by Spoonflower
www.spoonflower.com

FOOD: BEYOND THE CAKE
Mini cheesecakes:
One Girl Cookies
www.onegirlcookies.com

Cake pops:
Haute So Sweet!
www.hautesosweet.com

Acrylic heart topper:
Little Cat Design Co.
http://littlecatdesignco.com

Red fondant cupcake toppers:
Candy Clay Cupcakes
www.candyclaycupcakes.com

Mini donuts:
Green Mountain Mini Baked
www.etsy.com/shop /GreenMntMiniBaked

Cake cups:
Bee's Knees Baking Co.
www.beeskneesbakingco.com

Pie:
Four and Twenty Blackbirds
www.birdsblack.com

Flag toppers:
Shop Sweet Lulu
www.shopsweetlulu.com

STYLING: AISLE RUNNERS
Marbled aisle runner:
Minted
www.minted.com

Ombré initialed aisle runner:
custom design, printed by Spoonflower
www.spoonflower.com

Floral aisle runner:
custom design, printed by Spoonflower
www.spoonflower.com

Geometric aisle runner:
custom design, printed by Spoonflower
www.spoonflower.com

Flagging tape:
Tape Brothers
www.tapebrothers.com

Sequins:
Cartwright's Sequins
www.ccartwright.com

White chairs:
Taylor Creative
www.taylorcreativeinc.com

"ASK THE EXPERT" CONTRIBUTORS

A.a.B. Creates, page 122
www.alwaysabridesmaid.us

Blossom and Branch, page 96
http://blossomandbranch.com

Brooklyn Tailors, page 174
www.brooklyn-tailors.com

Cobblestone Catering, page 228
www.cobblestonecatering.com

Face Time Beauty, page 42
http://facetimebeauty.com

Gabriella New York Bridal Salon, page 146
www.gabriellanewyork.com

Nine Cakes, page 198
http://ninecakes.com

Paper + Cup, page 70
www.papercupdesign.com

Yellow/ Orange

FLOWERS: CEREMONY FLOWERS

Pegboard:
Collector NYC
http://collector-nyc.com

Florals:
Blossom and Branch
www.blossomandbranch.com

Clear chairs:
Taylor Creative
www.taylorcreativeinc.com

Himmeli ornaments
Me + She by Megin Sherry
www.etsy.com/shop
/meginsherry

FASHION: VEILS & FASCINATORS

Bird headpiece:
Leah C Millinery
http://shop.leahc.com

Veil with orchid:
Preston & Olivia
http://prestonandolivia.com

Orange floral crown:
Mignonne Handmade
www.etsy.com/shop
/mignonnehandmade

Yellow vintage veil with feather detail:
Jade Rose Designs
www.jaderoseblog.com

Classic yellow bubble veil:
Beatrice Couture Designs
http://shop
.beatricecouturedesigns.com

Neon orange blusher:
Jennifer Behr
www.jenniferbehr.com

Camisoles:
Journelle
www.journelle.com

PAPER: PROGRAMS

Animal-themed program:
INK+WIT, printed by Boxcar Press
http://inkandwit.com
www.boxcarpress.com

Fan programs:
Swiss Cottage Designs
www.swisscottagedesigns
.com

Accordion program:
Fourteen-Forty
www.1440nyc.com

Linens:
The Cloth Connection
www.clothconnection.com

FOOD: COLD DESSERTS

Popsicles:
Popbar
www.popbar.com

Ice cream accessories:
Shop Sweet Lulu
www.shopsweetlulu.com

STYLING: FAVORS TO KEEP

Tea towels:
custom design, printed by Spoonflower
www.spoonflower.com

Tote:
Maptote
http://maptote.com

Custom pencils:
The Carbon Crusader
www.etsy.com/shop
/thecarboncrusader

Custom pins:
Busy Beaver Button Co.
www.busybeaver.net

Soap favors:
Vice and Velvet
www.etsy.com/shop
/viceandvelvet

Temporary tattoos:
Tattly
http://tattly.com

Keytags:
Various Keytags
http://variouskeytags.com

Leather bags:
Baggu
https://baggu.com

Tangrams and XO's:
MAKEatx
http://makeatx.com

DIY: KEEPSAKE BOX

Linens:
Nüage Designs
www.nuagedesigns.com

Green

Plate selections:
Courtesy of Bloomingdales
www.bloomingdales.com

FLOWERS: CENTERPIECES

Flowers:
Blossom and Branch
www.blossomandbranch.com

FASHION: BRIDESMAIDS' DRESSES

Shoes:
Kate Spade
www.katespade.com

Bridesmaids' dresses:
Ann Taylor
www.anntaylor.com

J. Crew
www.jcrew.com/index.jsp

Donna Morgan
www.donna-morgan.com

Jenny Yoo
www.jennyyoo.com/splash
.html

Adrianna Papell
www.adriannapapell.com

PAPER: GUEST BOOKS

Custom stamps:
custom design, made by Stampworx2000.biz
http://stampworx2000.biz

FOOD: CAKE TOPPERS & SERVING ACCESSORIES

Solid green cake stand:
Bauer Pottery
http://bauerpottery.com

Green cake server and knife:
Leif
www.leifshop.com

White cake server and knife:
BHLDN
www.bhldn.com

Mint green cake stand:
Sarah's Stands
http://sarahsstands.com

Mini green base stand:
Jansen+co
www.jansenco.nl

Green cake stand cling:
Shop Sweet Lulu
www.shopsweetlulu.com

Multigarland cake topper:
Potter + Butler
www.etsy.com/shop
/PotterandButler

Felt-lettered garland:
Pipsqueak & Bean
www.etsy.com/shop
/pipsqueakandbean

Couple cake topper:
Together Forever
www.etsy.com/shop
/togetherforever

Silhouette cake topper:
Simply Silhouettes Weddings
www.etsy.com/shop
/Silhouetteweddings

Fondant wreath:
Signe Sugar
http://signesugar.bigcartel
.com

Linens:
Nüage Designs
www.nuagedesigns.com

STYLING: SIGNAGE
Small food signage:
Julie Song Ink
www.juliesongink.com

Round "Mr. & Mrs." signs:
Host & Toast
www.etsy.com/shop
/hostandtoaststudio

Calligraphy portrait:
Stephanie Fishwick
www.stephaniefishwick.com

Bunting:
Liddabits
www.etsy.com/shop/liddabits

Cupcake liners for wreaths:
Sweet Estelle
www.etsy.com/shop
/sweetestelle

Cupcake wreath calligraphy:
Neither Snow
www.neithersnow.com

Light box and oversized
X & O:
Surface Grooves
http://surfacegrooves.com

Paper wrap:
Egg Press
http://eggpress.com

Banner:
Happy Menocal
www.happymenocal.com

Blue/Purple

FLOWERS:
BOUTONNIERES
Floral boutonnieres:
Blossom and Branch
www.blossomandbranch.com

Plaid and polka-dot
boutonniere:
Sara Monica
www.etsy.com/shop
/SaraMonicaLLC

Striped boutonniere:
VanCocoa Designs
www.etsy.com/shop
/VanCocoaDesigns

FASHION: SHOES
Glitter heart shoe clips:
Polly McGeary
www.etsy.com/shop
/PollyMcGeary

Men's shoes:
Cole Haan
www.colehaan.com

Women's shoes:
J. Crew
www.jcrew.com

Kate Spade
www.katespade.com

Charles David
www.charlesdavid.com

PAPER:
CALLIGRAPHY
Calligraphy:
May-belle
www.may-belle.com

Betsy Dunlap
http://bdunlap.blogspot.com

Neither Snow
www.neithersnow.com

Linea Carta
http://linea-carta.com

Love, Jenna
http://lovejennacalligraphy
.com

Paperfinger
www.paperfinger.com

Stephanie Fishwick
http://design.
stephaniefishwick.com

FOOD: SIGNATURE
COCKTAILS &
ACCOUTREMENTS
Paper straws:
The Sugar Diva
www.thesugardiva.com

Custom name straws:
Krazy Straws
www.krazystraws.com

Glittery tasseled stirrers:
Sparkle Motion Decor
www.etsy.com/shop
/SparkleMotionDecor

STYLING:
GARLANDS
Forever garland:
Banter Banner
http://banter-banner.
myshopify.com

Tissue fringe garland:
The Flair Exchange
www.etsy.com/shop
/TheFlairExchange

DIY: CHOCOLATE DÉCOR
Blue cake stand:
Fishs Eddy
www.fishseddy.com

Cakes:
Nine Cakes
www.ninecakes.com

White

FLOWERS: FLORAL HEADPIECES
Floral comb:
Mignonne Handmade
www.etsy.com/shop /mignonnehandmade

White silk floral headpiece with veil:
Jennifer Behr
www.jenniferbehr.com

White individual floral hairpins:
Hushed Commotion
http://hushedcommotion.com

Real floral headpieces:
Blossom and Branch
www.blossomandbranch.com

Camisoles:
Journelle
www.journelle.com

FASHION: WEDDING DRESSES
Flower backdrop:
Balushka
www.etsy.com/shop/balushka

Wedding dresses:
Johanna Johnson, courtesy of Gabriella New York Bridal Salon
www.johannajohnson.com
www.gabriellanewyork.com

Reem Acra, courtesy of Gabriella New York Bridal Salon
http://reemacra.com
www.gabriellanewyork.com

Ann Taylor
www.anntaylor.com

J. Crew
www.jcrew.com

Christos
http://christosbridal.com

Amsale
http://amsale.com

PAPER: SAVE-THE-DATES
Paper picado:
Ay Mujer
www.etsy.com/shop/AyMujer

Personalized leather tags:
Cocos Heaven
www.etsy.com/shop /cocosheaven

Blind embossed:
Elum
www.elumdesigns.com

Wax seal:
WaxSeals.com
www.waxseals.com

Polka-dot wallpaper:
Chasing Paper
www.chasingpaper.com

FOOD: DESSERT BAR
Animal cake stands:
Imm Living
www.imm-living.com

White platters:
CB2
www.cb2.com

Mini donuts:
Doughnuttery
www.doughnuttery.com

Cupcakes w/fondant toppers:
Candy Clay Cupcakes
www.candyclaycupcakes.com

Hexagon cookies:
Früute
www.fruute.com

White truffles:
Vosges Haut-Chocolat
www.vosgeschocolate.com

Linens:
Nüage Designs
www.nuagedesigns.com

STYLING: TABLE NUMBERS
Acrylic table numbers:
Little Cat Design Co.
http://littlecatdesignco.com

Robot:
Areaware
www.areaware.com

Clock:
West Elm
www.westelm.com

Centerpiece:
Blossom and Branch
www.blossomandbranch.com

Black

FLOWERS: DECORATING YOUR BOUQUET
Bouquet ribbons and tassels:
MJ Trim
www.mjtrim.com

Bouquets:
Blossom and Branch
www.blossomandbranch.com

Backdrop:
Minted
www.minted.com

FASHION: GROOM & GROOMSMEN
Cufflinks and tie clips:
Cufflinks.com
www.cufflinks.com

Shirt with heart:
J. Crew
www.jcrew.com

Men's suit and tux:
Brooklyn Tailors
www.brooklyn-tailors.com

Socks:
Happy Socks
www.happysocks.com

Shoes:
Jeffery West
www.jeffery-west.us

PAPER: INVITATIONS & PRINTING TECHNIQUES
Printerette
www.printerettepress.com

Invitations:
Mr. Boddington
www.mrboddington.com

MaeMae Paperie
www.maemaepaperie.com

Thoughtful Day
http://thoughtfulday.com

Cheree Berry Paper
http://chereeberrypaper.com

Egg Press
http://eggpress.com

Ladyfingers Letterpress
http://ladyfingersletterpress
.com

FOOD: EDIBLE FAVORS

Bow-tie piñatas:
Vintage Baby Doll
www.etsy.com/shop
/Vintagebabydoll

Dipped pretzel sticks:
Fatty Sundays
www.fattysundays.com

Personalized candies:
Papabubble
http://papabubble.com

Candy:
Sugarfina
www.sugarfina.com

Candy Warehouse
www.candywarehouse.com

Paper candy containers:
My Crazy Hands
www.etsy.com/shop
/myCrazyHands

Cupcake boxes and clear
boxes with striped band:
Tableau Party
www.tableauparty.com

Black macaron boxes:
SnD Supply
www.etsy.com/shop
/SnDSupply

Black and white cookies:
Merlino Baking Co. from
Seattle Gourmet Foods
www.seattlegourmetfoods
.com

Chocolate bars:
Mast Brothers Chocolate
http://mastbrothers.com

STYLING: RING PILLOWS

Ring bowl:
Paloma's Nest
http://palomasnest.com

Wooden diamond box:
Areaware
www.areaware.com

Balloon dog:
Brooklyn Balloon Company
http://brooklynballoon
company.com

Gray

Escort card calligraphy:
Linea Carta
http://linea-carta.com

FLOWERS: CORSAGES

Real floral corsages:
Blossom and Branch
www.blossomandbranch.com

Fabric corsages:
When Love Happens
www.etsy.com/shop
/WhenLoveHappens

Bridesmaids dress:
J. Crew
www.jcrew.com

Paper corsage:
Blooms in the Air
www.bloomsintheair.com

FASHION: BRIDAL ACCESSORIES

Floral sash:
When Love Happens
www.etsy.com/shop
/WhenLoveHappens

Ostrich feather clutch:
Sara C. Accessories
www.saracaccessories.com

Embroidered polka-dot clutch
Allisa Jacobs
www.etsy.com/shop
/allisajacobs

Gray lace shrug and marabou
jacket:
The Wedding Dresser
http://theweddingdresser
.com/index.html

Wedding dress:
J. Crew
www.jcrew.com

PAPER: MENUS

Napkin menu:
custom design, printed by
Spoonflower
www.spoonflower.com

Gray plates:
West Elm
www.westelm.com

Oversized illustrated menu:
Swiss Cottage Designs
www.swisscottagedesigns
.com

Watercolor plate menu:
Julie Song Ink
www.juliesongink.com

Linens:
The Cloth Connection
www.clothconnection.com

FOOD: WEDDING CAKES

Cakes:
Nine Cakes
www.ninecakes.com

Calligraphy signs:
Fourteen-Forty
www.1440nyc.com

Linens:
Nüage Designs
www.nuagedesigns.com

STYLING: PHOTO DISPLAY

Gray paper mat:
Minted
www.minted.com

Frames:
West Elm
www.westelm.com

Calligraphy decal on cloche:
Neither Snow
www.neithersnow.com

Guest book:
Izola
www.izola.com

Metallic

FLOWERS: CREATIVE CENTERPIECES
Faceted wood candlesticks:
PELLE Designs
www.pelledesigns.com

Gold bowl:
CB2
www.cb2.com

Gold lanterns:
Oriental Trading Company
www.orientaltrading.com

Long wood votive
candleholder:
Host & Toast
www.etsy.com/shop
/hostandtoaststudio

Paper fortune cookies:
Republic of Party
www.etsy.com/shop
/RepublicOfParty

Flatware:
West Elm
www.westelm.com

Linens:
The Cloth Connection
www.clothconnection.com

FASHION: JEWELRY
Bario Neal
http://bario-neal.com

Carla Caruso
Jerry Spaulding
Rebecca Overmann
Megan Thorne
Caroline Ellen
Annie Fensterstock
Marian Maurer
Sara McGuire
all courtesy of The Clay Pot
www.clay-pot.com

Thomas Laine
www.thomaslaine.com

Nordstrom
http://shop.nordstrom.com

Erica Weiner
http://ericaweiner.com

Nicholas Liu
www.nicholas-liu.com

Jennifer Yi Jewelry
www.etsy.com/shop
/jenniferyijewelry

Donovan Smith
http://donovansmithdesign
.com

PAPER: SEATING CHARTS & ESCORT CARDS
Calligraphy on silver bow
poster:
Julie Song Ink
www.juliesongink.com

Place card calligraphy:
Linea Carta
www.linea-carta.com

Paper Finger
http://paperfinger.com

Julie Song
www.juliesongink.com

Kaleidoscope Calligraphy
http://kaleidoscopecalligraphy
.bizhosting.com

Betsy Dunlap
http://bdunlap.blogspot.com

Stephanie Fishwick
http://design.
stephaniefishwick.com

Patterned escort cards:
Sugar Paper
www.sugarpaper.com

FOOD: HORS D'OEUVRES PRESENTATION
Metallic platters:
West Elm
www.westelm.com

Acrylic tray with gold stripes:
The Pink Orange
http://thepinkorange.com

Food by:
Cobblestone Catering
www.cobblestonecatering
.com

STYLING: CELEBRATION
Sparklers, horns, confetti
popper:
TOPS Malibu
http://topsmalibu.com

Confetti bomb:
Knot + Bow
www.etsy.com/shop
/knotandbow

YAY balloons:
Poppies for Grace
www.poppiesforgrace.com

Confetti bar spoons:
Leif
www.leifshop.com

Confetti:
Confetti.com
www.confetti.com

Resources

Bake It Pretty
www.bakeitpretty.com

Confetti System
www.confettisystem.com

Dabney Lee
www.dabneylee.com

Forage
http://forage.bigcartel.com

Fox & Brie
www.etsy.com/shop
/FoxandBrie

Geronimo Balloons
http://geronimoballoons.com

Goose Grease
www.etsy.com/shop
/goosegrease

The Great Lakes Goods
www.thegreatlakes.bigcartel
.com

inkkit
www.etsy.com/shop/inkkit

Lovely
www.lovelybride.com

Luxe Lollipops
www.etsy.com/shop
/LuxeLollipops

M and J Trim
www.mjtrim.com

Melabo Wed
www.etsy.com/shop
/MelaboWed

New York Central Art
www.nycentralart.com

Paper Mart
www.papermart.com

Paper Presentation
www.paperpresentation.com

Paper Source
www.papersource.com

Papyrus
www.papyrusonline.com

The Pink Orange
www.thepinkorange.com

Purl Soho
www.purlsoho.com

Stone Fox Bride
www.stonefoxbride.com

Sucre Shop
www.sucreshop.com

The TomKat Studio
http://shoptomkat.com

Urbanic Paper Boutique
www.urbanicpaper.com

Yes Ma'am Paper + Goods
http://yesma.am

Index